# THE PRINCIPLES OF NOUTHETIC COUNSELING

DR. GREG WOOD

# The Principles of Nouthetic Counseling
By **Dr. Greg Wood**

# Table of Contents

Dedication .................................................................................... 1
Acknowledgments ...................................................................... 3
Preface ......................................................................................... 5
Chapter 1: The Biblical Basis of Counseling ............................ 7
Chapter 2: The Meaning of "Nouthetic" ................................ 11
Chapter 3: The Goal of Nouthetic Counseling — Transformation into Christlikeness ................................................................. 15
Chapter 4: Confrontation in Love ......................................... 21
Chapter 5: The Role of Scripture in Counseling .................. 27
Chapter 6: The Work of the Holy Spirit in Counseling ....... 33
Chapter 7: Personal Responsibility in Change ..................... 39
Chapter 8: Hope in Christ as the Anchor of Counseling .... 45
Chapter 9: The Counselor's Life and Qualifications ........... 51
Chapter 10: Listening and Discernment ............................... 57
Chapter 11: Speaking the Truth in Love ............................... 63
Chapter 12: The Process of Change ...................................... 69
Chapter 13: Dealing with Anger ............................................ 75
Chapter 14: Overcoming Anxiety and Fear .......................... 81
Chapter 15: Breaking Free from Addictions ........................ 87
Chapter 16: Marriage and Family Issues .............................. 93
Chapter 17: Depression and Despair ..................................... 99
Chapter 18: Forgiveness and Reconciliation ...................... 105
Chapter 19: Counseling Through Grief and Loss .............. 111
Chapter 20: Counseling the Church Body ......................... 117
Chapter 21: Counseling in Times of Crisis ........................ 123
Chapter 22: Counseling and Spiritual Warfare .................. 129
Chapter 23: The Goal of Nouthetic Counseling: Christlikeness ........................................................................ 135
Chapter 24: The Eternal Perspective in Counseling .......... 141
Conclusion: The Sufficiency of Christ and His Word ....... 145

© 2025 Dr. Greg Wood
All rights reserved.

No part of this book may be reproduced, stored in a retrieval system, or transmitted in any form or by any means—electronic, mechanical, photocopying, recording, or otherwise—without prior written permission of the author, except for brief quotations in reviews or articles.

Unless otherwise indicated, all Scripture quotations are taken from the **New King James Version (NKJV)** of the Bible. Used by permission. All rights reserved.

Printed in the United States of America.

# Dedication

To my Lord and Savior, Jesus Christ, the Wonderful Counselor, whose Word is sufficient and whose grace is transforming.

And to those who long to bring His truth and hope into the lives of the hurting—may this book serve as a tool in your hands for His glory.

# Acknowledgments

I am deeply grateful to God for His wisdom, mercy, and the truth of His Word, which is sufficient for all matters of life and godliness.

To my family, whose love, support, and prayers have sustained me in ministry.

To fellow pastors, counselors, and teachers who have modeled biblical faithfulness and reminded me of the calling to "admonish the unruly, encourage the fainthearted, and help the weak" (1 Thessalonians 5:14).

To every student of Scripture and counseling—may you never lose sight of Christ, the Wonderful Counselor.

# Preface

This book was written out of a conviction that **God's Word is sufficient** to meet the deepest needs of the human heart. In an age when counseling is often shaped by psychology and human philosophy, it is vital to return to the **biblical foundation of soul care.**

Nouthetic Counseling—sometimes called "biblical counseling"—is not a new method but a recovery of what Scripture has always taught: admonishing, correcting, and encouraging one another with God's truth so that we may grow in Christlikeness.

The chapters in this book are designed to provide both a theological foundation and practical guidance. They address real struggles—anger, fear, anxiety, addiction, grief, depression—and apply the eternal truths of Scripture.

My prayer is that this book will equip pastors, counselors, and lay believers to minister the Word faithfully, offering true hope to the broken and leading them toward the ultimate goal of all counseling: **conformity to Christ.**

# Chapter 1: The Biblical Basis of Counseling

**Introduction**

Every generation faces struggles of the human soul—fear, anger, despair, broken relationships, guilt, and shame. Modern psychology offers many theories, yet the Bible declares that **God's Word is sufficient** to address the deepest needs of the human heart. Nouthetic Counseling, first championed by Dr. Jay Adams, is firmly grounded in the conviction that **Scripture alone is the authoritative, complete, and trustworthy guide for helping people change.**

The purpose of this chapter is to establish that counseling is not a man-made invention but a **biblical mandate**, rooted in God's Word, carried out by God's people, and empowered by God's Spirit.

**1. Scripture Is Sufficient for Counseling**

The cornerstone of Nouthetic Counseling is the conviction that **the Bible is enough**. Every believer must begin with this truth:

"All Scripture is given by inspiration of God, and is profitable for doctrine, for reproof, for correction, for instruction in righteousness, that the man of God may be complete, thoroughly equipped for every good work."

—2 Timothy 3:16–17 (NKJV)

Notice the four uses of Scripture:

- **Doctrine** – What is right (truth).
- **Reproof** – What is wrong (exposing sin).
- **Correction** – How to get right (restoration).
- **Instruction in righteousness** – How to stay right (ongoing growth).

Paul affirms that the Bible is sufficient to make the believer **"complete"** and **"equipped"** for *every good work*, including the work of counseling. There is no category of human struggle outside God's reach.

**Supporting Scriptures:**

- Psalm 19:7–11 – God's Word revives the soul, gives wisdom, rejoices the heart, enlightens the eyes.
- Hebrews 4:12 – The Word is alive, piercing to the thoughts and intentions of the heart.
- 2 Peter 1:3 – God has given us *all things* pertaining to life and godliness through His promises.

**Application:** When someone comes for counseling, the counselor must begin not with theories of Freud, Jung, or secular psychology, but with God's inspired Word. To do otherwise is to offer breadless stones to hungry souls (cf. Matthew 7:9).

## 2. Counseling Is the Responsibility of the Church

Biblical counseling is not reserved for professional "experts." The early church understood that **all believers are called to admonish, encourage, and strengthen one another**.

"Now I myself am confident concerning you, my brethren, that you also are full of goodness, filled with all knowledge, able also to admonish one another."
—Romans 15:14

Paul assumed that ordinary Christians, filled with the Spirit and the Word, were **competent to counsel.** Counseling, therefore, belongs to the life of the local church.

**Supporting Scriptures:**

- Galatians 6:1–2 – "Brethren, if a man is overtaken in any trespass, you who are spiritual restore such a one in a spirit of gentleness... Bear one another's burdens, and so fulfill the law of Christ."

# THE PRINCIPLES OF NOUTHETIC COUNSELING

- Colossians 3:16 – "Let the word of Christ dwell in you richly... teaching and admonishing one another in all wisdom."
- Hebrews 10:24–25 – We are to "stir up one another to love and good works" and not neglect assembling together.

**Application:** Every believer should see himself as part of God's "counseling team." Whether in the pulpit, small group, or personal conversation, God calls His people to counsel one another with His Word.

### 3. The Biblical Concept of "Nouthetic" Counseling

The term *nouthetic* comes from the Greek word **noutheteo**, meaning *to admonish, warn, instruct, or correct with the goal of change.* This word appears several times in the New Testament:

- Acts 20:31 – Paul admonished the Ephesian elders "night and day with tears."
- Colossians 1:28 – Paul's mission: "Him we proclaim, warning (*noutheteo*) every man and teaching every man... that we may present every man mature in Christ."
- 1 Thessalonians 5:14 – "Now we exhort you, brethren, warn those who are unruly, comfort the fainthearted, uphold the weak, be patient with all."

Nouthetic counseling, then, is not harsh rebuke but **loving, truth-filled admonition aimed at transformation**. It is **personal, directive, and biblical**—addressing sin, offering hope, and pointing the counselee to Christ.

**Application:** True counseling does not simply listen without direction, nor does it excuse sin. Instead, it lovingly confronts and redirects, much like a shepherd guiding sheep away from danger and into safe pastures.

### 4. Christ as the Wonderful Counselor

The foundation of counseling is not a method but a Person: Jesus Christ, the **Wonderful Counselor** (Isaiah 9:6). His words bring healing, His presence brings peace, His Spirit brings transformation.

- John 14:26 – The Holy Spirit is our Counselor and Teacher, reminding us of Christ's words.
- Matthew 11:28–30 – Jesus invites the weary and burdened to find rest in Him.
- Luke 4:18 – Christ declared His mission was to heal the brokenhearted and set the captives free.

**Application:** All true counseling must be **Christ-centered.** It is not about self-fulfillment but about bringing people to Christ for forgiveness, hope, and new life.

**Conclusion**

Nouthetic Counseling is **not an optional ministry** but a **biblical mandate.** Scripture is sufficient, the church is responsible, *noutheteo* is the model, and Christ is the Counselor.

The counselor's task is not to entertain, philosophize, or speculate—but to **open God's Word, apply it with love, and walk alongside the struggler until he or she is restored and strengthened in Christ.**

**Reflection Questions for Chapter 1**

1. According to 2 Timothy 3:16–17, how does Scripture equip us for the work of counseling?
2. Why must counseling belong to the church and not only to professionals?
3. How does the Greek concept of *noutheteo* shape our understanding of counseling?
4. In what ways does Christ Himself model perfect counseling?
5. What areas in your own life might need "nouthetic admonition" from Scripture today?

# Chapter 2: The Meaning of "Nouthetic" (Admonition, Warning, Instruction)

**Introduction**

The word *Nouthetic* may sound unfamiliar to many, yet it comes directly from the language of the New Testament. The Greek word **noutheteo** (νουθετέω) forms the foundation of what we call **Nouthetic Counseling**. This term captures the essence of biblical counseling: lovingly admonishing, warning, and instructing others with God's truth in order to bring about genuine transformation.

In this chapter, we will explore the **meaning, biblical usage, and practical application** of *noutheteo*, and how it shapes the very heart of Christian counseling.

**1. The Root of the Word "Nouthetic"**

The word **noutheteo** is a compound word:

- *nous* = mind, understanding, or inner thoughts
- *tithemi* = to place, put, or set

Thus, *noutheteo* literally means **"to put into the mind."** It implies **teaching, admonishing, or warning with intent**—not merely giving information but aiming at heart-level change.

This shows that counseling is not casual conversation; it is **intentional instruction designed to reshape thinking and behavior** according to God's truth.

**2. The New Testament Use of "Noutheteo"**

The word *noutheteo* appears several times in Scripture. Let's examine its usage and what it teaches us about counseling:

**a. Acts 20:31 – Paul's Pastoral Example**

"Therefore watch, and remember that for three years I did not cease to warn (*noutheteo*) everyone night and day with tears."

Paul's admonition was **persistent, personal,** and **passionate**. He didn't just deliver doctrine; he warned with tears, showing deep compassion. Counseling requires the same: firm truth delivered with tender love.

### b. Romans 15:14 – The Church's Responsibility

"Now I myself am confident concerning you, my brethren, that you also are full of goodness, filled with all knowledge, able also to admonish (*noutheteo*) one another."

Paul affirms that ordinary Christians, filled with God's Spirit and knowledge of His Word, are competent to admonish one another. Counseling is not limited to pastors or specialists—it is the work of the whole body of Christ.

### c. 1 Corinthians 4:14 – Admonition with Love

"I do not write these things to shame you, but as my beloved children I warn (*noutheteo*) you."

Here Paul clarifies the spirit of admonition. It is not to **shame** but to **lovingly warn**. True biblical counseling never crushes a person but directs them toward healing and holiness.

### d. Colossians 1:28 – The Goal of Maturity

"Him we proclaim, warning (*noutheteo*) every man and teaching every man in all wisdom, that we may present every man perfect in Christ Jesus."

Paul's mission was twofold: **proclaim Christ and admonish with wisdom.** The goal of counseling is not simply problem-solving but **presenting people mature in Christ.**

### e. 1 Thessalonians 5:14 – Different People, Different Needs

"Now we exhort you, brethren, warn (*noutheteo*) those who are unruly, comfort the fainthearted, uphold the weak, be patient with all."

Notice how admonition is part of a broader ministry. Some need **warning**, others need **comfort**, others need **support.** Nouthetic counseling requires discernment—knowing when to correct, when to comfort, and when to encourage.

### 3. The Spirit of Nouthetic Counseling

While *noutheteo* involves admonition, it is never harsh or self-righteous. Three qualities must always shape it:

1. **Truthful** – Rooted in the Word of God (John 17:17).
2. **Loving** – Flowing from compassion and care (Ephesians 4:15).
3. **Hopeful** – Always pointing to the power of Christ to change lives (Romans 15:13).

Paul modeled this balance—firm in truth, but tender in spirit, counseling with tears when necessary (Acts 20:31).

### 4. Nouthetic vs. Secular Counseling

Secular counseling often seeks to **ease pain, boost self-esteem, or manage behavior**, while nouthetic counseling seeks **real transformation** through repentance and renewal.

- **Secular model:** "You need to accept yourself as you are."
- **Nouthetic model:** "You must turn from sin and grow into Christlikeness." (Ephesians 4:22–24)

This distinction is critical. The goal is not simply to feel better but to **become holy**.

### 5. Practical Application of Nouthetic Admonition

How does *noutheteo* work in real counseling situations?

- **When confronting sin** – (Galatians 6:1) restore gently, but clearly point to repentance.
- **When addressing fear or anxiety** – (Philippians 4:6–7) admonish toward prayer and trust in God's promises.
- **When guiding families** – (Ephesians 6:4) fathers are told to "bring up" children in the discipline and **admonition (*noutheteo*) of the Lord."

- **When discipling believers** – admonition becomes part of everyday discipleship, equipping others to grow in Christ.

## Conclusion

The word *noutheteo* teaches us that counseling is not passive listening but **active, loving instruction that brings about change.** It involves **warning, guiding, and correcting**, always with the goal of maturity in Christ.

The counselor must hold together **truth and grace**—a faithful application of God's Word, delivered with compassion, and grounded in the hope of the gospel.

### Reflection Questions for Chapter 2

1. What does the literal meaning of *noutheteo* teach us about the nature of biblical counseling?
2. How does Paul's example in Acts 20:31 model the balance of truth and compassion?
3. Why is admonition necessary for spiritual growth, and how can it be done in love?
4. How does Colossians 1:28 shape the ultimate goal of counseling?
5. What differences stand out between secular counseling and nouthetic counseling?

# Chapter 3: The Goal of Nouthetic Counseling — Transformation into Christlikeness

**Introduction**

What is the aim of counseling? In secular psychology, the goals vary—self-actualization, personal peace, improved coping skills, or maximizing one's potential. While some of these sound helpful, they fall far short of God's purpose.

In Nouthetic Counseling, the goal is not temporary relief but **lasting transformation**. This transformation is not defined by worldly success or inner comfort but by becoming more like **Jesus Christ**.

"For whom He foreknew, He also predestined to be conformed to the image of His Son."
—Romans 8:29

This verse sets the trajectory for the believer's entire life. Counseling, discipleship, and the Christian walk all point toward this end: **Christlikeness**.

**1. God's Eternal Purpose: Conformity to Christ**

From eternity past, God's purpose was to shape His children into the likeness of His Son.

- **Romans 8:29–30** – God predestined us to be conformed to Christ's image, called us, justified us, and will glorify us.
- **Ephesians 1:4** – God chose us before the foundation of the world to be holy and blameless.
- **1 Thessalonians 4:3** – "This is the will of God, your sanctification."

The counselor must constantly hold this before the counselee: God is not interested in simply making life easier—He is committed to making His children holy.

**Application:** When counselees struggle, remind them that their pain is not wasted. God uses trials to shape us:

- James 1:2–4 – Trials test our faith and produce maturity.
- Hebrews 12:10–11 – God disciplines us so we may share His holiness.

**2. Transformation: The Renewing of the Mind**

Paul contrasts two paths: conformity to the world or transformation into Christlikeness.

"Do not be conformed to this world, but be transformed by the renewing of your mind."
—Romans 12:2

Transformation (*metamorphoo*) means a complete change in form. Just as a caterpillar becomes a butterfly, God calls us to radical inward renewal that produces outward fruit.

**Supporting Scriptures:**

- **Ephesians 4:22–24** – Put off the old man, be renewed, put on the new man.
- **Colossians 3:9–10** – The new self is renewed in knowledge after Christ.
- **Psalm 119:105** – God's Word is a lamp to our feet and a light to our path.
- **Joshua 1:8** – Meditating on God's Word leads to obedience and success.

**Application in Counseling:**

- A counselee filled with fear must renew the mind with

promises of God's presence (Isaiah 41:10; Matthew 28:20).
- A counselee battling shame must renew the mind with God's full forgiveness (1 John 1:9; Psalm 103:12).
- A counselee trapped in bitterness must renew the mind with Christ's command to forgive (Matthew 6:14–15; Colossians 3:13).

### 3. The Put Off / Put On Pattern

Paul repeatedly describes transformation as a cycle: **putting off sin, renewing the mind, and putting on righteousness.**

"That you put off, concerning your former conduct, the old man... and be renewed in the spirit of your mind, and... put on the new man which was created according to God, in true righteousness and holiness."
—Ephesians 4:22–24

**Examples with Expanded Scripture:**

- **Anger**
    - Put off: "Let all bitterness, wrath, anger... be put away from you" (Ephesians 4:31).
    - Renew: "Be swift to hear, slow to speak, slow to wrath" (James 1:19–20).
    - Put on: "Be kind to one another, tenderhearted, forgiving one another" (Ephesians 4:32).
- **Anxiety**
    - Put off: "Do not worry about your life" (Matthew 6:25).
    - Renew: "Cast all your care upon Him, for He cares for you" (1 Peter 5:7).
    - Put on: "Be anxious for nothing, but in everything by prayer and supplication... let your requests be made known to God" (Philippians 4:6–7).

- **Sexual Sin**
    - Put off: "Flee sexual immorality" (1 Corinthians 6:18).
    - Renew: "Your body is the temple of the Holy Spirit" (1 Corinthians 6:19–20).
    - Put on: "Present your bodies a living sacrifice, holy, acceptable to God" (Romans 12:1).
- **Bitterness and Unforgiveness**
    - Put off: "Looking carefully... lest any root of bitterness springing up cause trouble" (Hebrews 12:15).
    - Renew: "Forgive, just as God in Christ forgave you" (Colossians 3:13).
    - Put on: "Above all these things put on love, which is the bond of perfection" (Colossians 3:14).

**4. The Work of the Holy Spirit in Transformation**

No counselor can change a heart. True transformation is **the Spirit's work.**

- **John 16:8** – The Spirit convicts of sin, righteousness, and judgment.
- **Galatians 5:16–17** – Walk in the Spirit, and you will not fulfill the lusts of the flesh.
- **2 Corinthians 3:18** – We are transformed by the Spirit into Christ's image.
- **Romans 8:13–14** – By the Spirit we put to death the deeds of the body.

**Application for Counseling:**

- Encourage counselees to pray daily for the Spirit's help (Luke

11:13).
- Teach reliance on the Spirit, not self-effort (Zechariah 4:6).
- Point to the Spirit's fruit as evidence of growth: love, joy, peace, patience, kindness, goodness, faithfulness, gentleness, self-control (Galatians 5:22–23).

**5. The End Goal: Spiritual Maturity**

Counseling cannot stop at temporary relief—it must aim for maturity.

"Him we proclaim, warning every man and teaching every man... that we may present every man perfect in Christ Jesus."
—Colossians 1:28

Maturity is measured by:

- **Obedience** – "Teaching them to observe all that I commanded you" (Matthew 28:20).
- **Discernment** – "Solid food belongs to those who are of full age... who by reason of use have their senses exercised to discern both good and evil" (Hebrews 5:14).
- **Fruitfulness** – "By this My Father is glorified, that you bear much fruit" (John 15:8).
- **Love** – "Above all these things put on love" (Colossians 3:14).

**Application:** The counselor should ask: "Is this person learning to glorify God in thought, word, and deed?" That is the true measure of successful counseling.

**Conclusion**

The goal of Nouthetic Counseling is **not self-help, not temporary relief, not simply improved feelings.** The goal is the very thing for which God saved us: **Christlikeness.**

This means helping counselees...

- **See their sin clearly** through God's Word.
- **Renew their minds daily** with biblical truth.
- **Walk in new obedience** empowered by the Spirit.
- **Grow toward maturity** until Christ is formed in them (Galatians 4:19).

Only when counseling is rooted in this goal will it bear eternal fruit.

**Reflection Questions for Chapter 3**

1. How do Romans 8:29 and Ephesians 1:4 show God's eternal plan for Christlikeness?
2. What does Romans 12:2 teach about the necessity of renewing the mind?
3. Using Ephesians 4:22–24, explain the "put off, renew, put on" model. How does this apply to anger, anxiety, and bitterness?
4. Why is the Holy Spirit essential for true transformation (2 Corinthians 3:18; Galatians 5:16)?
5. How can a counselor measure whether a counselee is growing toward maturity in Christ?

# Chapter 4: Confrontation in Love

**Introduction**

One of the most misunderstood aspects of biblical counseling is the idea of **confrontation**. In the world, confrontation is often seen as hostile, judgmental, or harsh. But in Scripture, confrontation—when done biblically—is an act of **love and restoration**.

Nouthetic Counseling insists that truth must be spoken into people's lives. But it must always be truth wrapped in grace, with the goal of repentance, healing, and Christlikeness.

**1. Confrontation Is Rooted in Love**

Many avoid confrontation because they fear it will damage relationships. But the Bible teaches the opposite: **loving someone means caring enough to confront.**

- **Proverbs 27:5-6** – "Open rebuke is better than love carefully concealed. Faithful are the wounds of a friend, but the kisses of an enemy are deceitful."
- **Revelation 3:19** – "As many as I love, I rebuke and chasten. Therefore be zealous and repent."
- **Leviticus 19:17** – "You shall not hate your brother in your heart. You shall surely rebuke your neighbor, and not bear sin because of him."

**Application:** Avoiding confrontation may feel kinder in the moment, but it leaves a person trapped in sin. True love calls us to rescue, not remain silent.

**2. The Spirit of Gentle Restoration**

Confrontation is never about pride or superiority—it is about gentle restoration.

"Brethren, if a man is overtaken in any trespass, you who are spiritual restore such a one in a spirit of gentleness, considering yourself lest you also be tempted."
—Galatians 6:1

**Key truths in this verse:**

- **"Overtaken"** – The counselee may be trapped in sin unintentionally or in weakness.
- **"Restore"** – The goal is healing, like mending a broken bone.
- **"Gentleness"** – Harshness destroys; gentleness heals.
- **"Considering yourself"** – The counselor must remain humble, remembering his own weakness.

**Supporting Scriptures:**

- 2 Timothy 2:24–25 – The Lord's servant must not quarrel but gently instruct, hoping God grants repentance.
- James 5:19–20 – Turning a sinner from his error saves a soul from death.
- Matthew 12:20 – Jesus would not break a bruised reed or quench a smoldering wick—our confrontation must reflect His compassion.

### 3. The Biblical Process of Confrontation

Jesus gave a clear process for addressing sin in others.

"Moreover if your brother sins against you, go and tell him his fault between you and him alone. If he hears you, you have gained your brother. But if he will not hear, take with you one or two more... And if he refuses to hear them, tell it to the church."
—Matthew 18:15–17

**The Steps:**

1. **Private confrontation** – one-on-one, avoiding gossip.

# THE PRINCIPLES OF NOUTHETIC COUNSELING 23

2. **Small group confrontation** – with witnesses, if necessary.
3. **Church involvement** – if the person remains unrepentant.

This process demonstrates patience, love, and fairness. It seeks repentance at the earliest stage possible while protecting the purity of the church.

**Supporting Scriptures:**

- Luke 17:3 – "If your brother sins against you, rebuke him; and if he repents, forgive him."
- Titus 3:10 – Warn a divisive person twice, then avoid them if unrepentant.
- 1 Corinthians 5:1–5 – Paul instructs discipline in the church for unrepentant sin, so the person's spirit may be saved.

### 4. Speaking the Truth in Love

Confrontation must always balance **truth and love**.

"But, speaking the truth in love, may grow up in all things into Him who is the head—Christ."
—Ephesians 4:15

Both elements are necessary:

- **Truth without love** = harsh legalism.
- **Love without truth** = weak compromise.
- **Truth in love** = godly confrontation leading to growth.

**Supporting Scriptures:**

- Proverbs 12:18 – "The tongue of the wise promotes health."
- Colossians 4:6 – "Let your speech always be with grace, seasoned with salt."
- 1 Thessalonians 5:14 – "Warn the unruly, comfort the fainthearted, uphold the weak, be patient with all."

## 5. Confrontation Produces Godly Change

Though painful at times, biblical confrontation can lead to genuine repentance and healing.

"For godly sorrow produces repentance leading to salvation, not to be regretted; but the sorrow of the world produces death."
—2 Corinthians 7:10

**Case Example:**
Paul confronted the Corinthian church for tolerating sin (1 Corinthians 5). Later, in 2 Corinthians 2:6–8, he encouraged forgiveness and restoration for the repentant brother. Confrontation worked—it brought repentance, sorrow, and restoration.

**Supporting Scriptures:**

- Hebrews 12:11 – Discipline is painful but yields peaceable fruit of righteousness.
- Psalm 141:5 – "Let the righteous strike me; it shall be a kindness."
- Proverbs 9:8–9 – A wise person receives rebuke and grows wiser.

## 6. Practical Guidelines for Loving Confrontation

1. **Pray first** – Ask God for humility and the right words (James 1:5).
2. **Check your motives** – Are you confronting to restore, or to prove yourself right? (Galatians 6:1).
3. **Use Scripture** – Let God's Word, not personal opinion, guide the conversation (2 Timothy 3:16).
4. **Be specific** – Address clear issues, not vague feelings.
5. **Offer hope** – Remind them of God's grace and forgiveness (1 John 1:9).
6. **Be patient** – Change is often gradual (Philippians 1:6).

**Conclusion**

Confrontation in biblical counseling is not about winning arguments or exposing faults—it is about **lovingly rescuing a brother or sister from sin.** Done correctly, confrontation is one of the most powerful tools of God's grace, leading to repentance, healing, and restored fellowship.

True confrontation requires courage, but when wrapped in love and guided by Scripture, it becomes an instrument of Christ's redeeming work.

**Reflection Questions for Chapter 4**

1. Why is confrontation an essential part of biblical counseling?
2. How does Galatians 6:1 shape our attitude when we confront?
3. What steps does Jesus give in Matthew 18:15–17, and why are they important?
4. How do we balance truth and love when confronting someone?
5. How can confrontation, though painful, produce righteousness in the counselee?

# Chapter 5: The Role of Scripture in Counseling

**Introduction**

If counseling is about guiding people through struggles, then the most important question is: **What tool do we use?** The world leans on psychology, self-help, and human theories. But the Christian counselor has something infinitely greater—**the living and active Word of God.**

The Bible is not merely a source of encouragement; it is God's **authoritative, sufficient, and transformative Word.** Nouthetic Counseling rests entirely on the conviction that **Scripture alone provides the truth and power necessary for real and lasting change.**

**1. Scripture Is Inspired and Sufficient**

Paul states it plainly:

"All Scripture is given by inspiration of God, and is profitable for doctrine, for reproof, for correction, for instruction in righteousness, that the man of God may be complete, thoroughly equipped for every good work."

—2 Timothy 3:16–17

**Key truths here:**

- **Inspired** – "God-breathed," carrying His divine authority.
- **Profitable** – Useful for every area of life.
- **Comprehensive** – Equips the believer for *every good work,* including counseling.

**Supporting Scriptures:**

- **Psalm 19:7–11** – God's law revives the soul, makes the simple wise, rejoices the heart, enlightens the eyes.
- **2 Peter 1:3–4** – God's promises give us *all things* pertaining

to life and godliness.
- **Hebrews 4:12** – The Word is living and powerful, discerning thoughts and intentions.

**Application:** Counselors must be convinced that no human wisdom compares to the wisdom of God's Word. If the Bible is sufficient, then our counseling must be biblical from beginning to end.

## 2. Scripture Exposes the Heart

Human problems are not merely external; they are rooted in the **heart.** Only Scripture can pierce deep enough to expose what is hidden.

- **Hebrews 4:12** – God's Word is sharper than a sword, dividing soul and spirit, judging the thoughts and intents of the heart.
- **Jeremiah 17:9–10** – The heart is deceitful above all things; God alone searches and tests it.
- **Proverbs 20:5** – "Counsel in the heart of man is like deep water, but a man of understanding will draw it out."

### Application in Counseling:

- A counselee angry at others may be harboring pride or unforgiveness—Scripture reveals this.
- A counselee struggling with despair may be believing lies about God's goodness—Scripture exposes those lies.
- A counselee battling addiction may have an idolatrous heart—Scripture uncovers false worship.

## 3. Scripture Corrects and Restores

# THE PRINCIPLES OF NOUTHETIC COUNSELING 29

The Word not only exposes sin—it also **corrects and restores.**

- **Psalm 119:9** – "How can a young man cleanse his way? By taking heed according to Your word."
- **John 17:17** – "Sanctify them by Your truth. Your word is truth."
- **James 1:22–25** – The Word is a mirror showing us who we are, but blessing comes when we act on it.

**Application in Counseling:**

- Scripture corrects lies with truth (John 8:31–32).
- Scripture corrects sinful habits with godly patterns (Ephesians 4:22–24).
- Scripture restores broken people by pointing them to the forgiveness and grace found in Christ (1 John 1:9; Psalm 51).

**4. Scripture Provides Hope**

People often come to counseling feeling hopeless. God's Word breathes hope into weary hearts.

- **Romans 15:4** – "Whatever things were written before were written for our learning, that we through the patience and comfort of the Scriptures might have hope."
- **Lamentations 3:21–23** – "This I recall to my mind, therefore I have hope: Through the LORD's mercies we are not consumed, because His compassions fail not."
- **Psalm 130:5** – "I wait for the LORD, my soul waits, and in His word I do hope."

**Application in Counseling:** The counselor must not only warn against sin but also infuse the counselee with the hope of God's promises. Every problem, no matter how dark, has an answer and a hope in Christ.

### 5. Scripture Gives Practical Wisdom

The Bible is not abstract—it gives clear, practical wisdom for everyday struggles.

- **Anger** – Proverbs 15:1; James 1:19–20.
- **Fear** – Isaiah 41:10; Matthew 6:34.
- **Marriage** – Ephesians 5:22–33; Colossians 3:18–21.
- **Work** – Colossians 3:23; Proverbs 14:23.
- **Finances** – Proverbs 22:7; 1 Timothy 6:6–10.
- **Speech** – Ephesians 4:29; Proverbs 18:21.

**Application:** The counselor's role is to guide the counselee to specific passages that address their struggles. Scripture is not only for worship—it is for **life application.**

### 6. Scripture Transforms Through the Gospel

At its heart, the Bible is about Jesus Christ. Real transformation happens when the counselee not only learns verses but sees how every Scripture points to Christ's redeeming work.

- **Luke 24:27** – Jesus explained that all Scripture points to Him.
- **2 Corinthians 5:17** – "If anyone is in Christ, he is a new creation."
- **Romans 1:16** – The gospel is the power of God for salvation to everyone who believes.
- **Titus 2:11–12** – God's grace trains us to renounce ungodliness and live godly lives.

**Application:** Every counseling session must ultimately point the person to Christ—His cross for forgiveness, His resurrection for hope, and His Spirit for power.

### 7. The Counselor's Confidence in Scripture

The counselor's authority does not come from skill, personality, or knowledge of psychology. It comes from faithfully applying the Word of God.

- **Isaiah 55:10–11** – God's Word does not return void but accomplishes His purpose.
- **1 Corinthians 2:4–5** – Paul did not rely on persuasive words of human wisdom but on the Spirit and power of God.
- **1 Thessalonians 2:13** – The Word of God works effectively in those who believe.

**Application:** The counselor must approach every session with confidence—not in themselves, but in the living Word that brings change.

### Conclusion

The role of Scripture in counseling is central and irreplaceable. The Bible is **sufficient, penetrating, corrective, hope-giving, practical, and Christ-centered.** Without Scripture, counseling may comfort temporarily, but it cannot transform eternally.

The counselor's task is to **open the Scriptures**, help the counselee see their heart in its light, and apply the gospel for true transformation.

### Reflection Questions for Chapter 5

1. How does 2 Timothy 3:16–17 prove the sufficiency of Scripture for counseling?
2. Why is the Bible uniquely able to expose the heart (Hebrews 4:12)?
3. How can Scripture both correct and restore a struggling

believer?
4. What role does hope from the Scriptures play in counseling the discouraged?
5. How does every counseling situation ultimately connect back to the gospel of Christ?

# Chapter 6: The Work of the Holy Spirit in Counseling

**Introduction**

No counselor, no matter how wise or experienced, has the power to change a human heart. Techniques, strategies, and advice can bring temporary relief, but true transformation is the work of the **Holy Spirit.**

Biblical counseling depends not on the wisdom of man but on the power of God. The Holy Spirit is the **Counselor, Comforter, Teacher, and Transformer** who brings conviction of sin, assurance of forgiveness, and the power for new life. Without the Spirit's presence and power, Nouthetic Counseling is powerless.

**1. The Holy Spirit as the Divine Counselor**

Jesus promised His disciples the **Helper (Paraklētos)**—the One who comes alongside to comfort and guide.

"And I will pray the Father, and He will give you another Helper, that He may abide with you forever—the Spirit of truth."
—John 14:16–17

**The Spirit's Role:**

- **Comforter** – He strengthens and consoles the brokenhearted (John 14:26–27).
- **Teacher** – He brings God's truth to remembrance (John 14:26).
- **Guide** – He leads us into all truth (John 16:13).

**Application in Counseling:** The human counselor is only an instrument; the Spirit is the true Counselor working in both the counselor and the counselee.

**2. The Spirit Convicts of Sin**

Real change begins when the Spirit convicts the heart of sin. Without conviction, people will excuse, justify, or minimize their wrongdoing.

"And when He has come, He will convict the world of sin, and of righteousness, and of judgment."
—John 16:8

**Supporting Scriptures:**

- Acts 2:37 – After Peter preached, the people were "cut to the heart" by the Spirit's conviction.
- Romans 3:20 – Through the law comes knowledge of sin, applied by the Spirit.
- Hebrews 3:7–8 – The Spirit warns: "Today, if you hear His voice, do not harden your hearts."

**Application:** Counselors should pray for the Spirit to open blind eyes and soften hard hearts. It is not arguments or persuasion that produce repentance, but the Spirit's conviction.

### 3. The Spirit Gives New Life

Counseling without the Spirit is like trying to reform the dead. The Spirit alone brings new birth and spiritual life.

- **John 3:5–6** – "Unless one is born of water and the Spirit, he cannot enter the kingdom of God."
- **Titus 3:5** – "He saved us... through the washing of regeneration and renewing of the Holy Spirit."
- **2 Corinthians 5:17** – In Christ we are a new creation, made possible by the Spirit.

# THE PRINCIPLES OF NOUTHETIC COUNSELING

**Application:** A counselee enslaved to sin does not need behavior modification but spiritual regeneration. The Spirit creates a new heart that desires holiness (Ezekiel 36:26–27).

### 4. The Spirit Produces Transformation

The Spirit not only gives life—He changes us progressively into Christ's image.

"But we all, with unveiled face, beholding as in a mirror the glory of the Lord, are being transformed into the same image... by the Spirit of the Lord."

—2 Corinthians 3:18

**Supporting Scriptures:**

- Galatians 5:16 – "Walk in the Spirit, and you shall not fulfill the lust of the flesh."
- Romans 8:13–14 – By the Spirit we put to death the deeds of the body.
- Philippians 2:13 – God works in us through His Spirit to will and to act according to His purpose.

**Application:** The Spirit enables believers to overcome sinful patterns, replacing them with godly fruit.

### 5. The Fruit of the Spirit as Evidence of Change

True counseling results in Spirit-produced fruit.

- **Galatians 5:22–23** – "The fruit of the Spirit is love, joy, peace, longsuffering, kindness, goodness, faithfulness, gentleness, self-control."
- **Romans 5:5** – The Spirit pours out God's love in our hearts.
- **Colossians 1:10–11** – The Spirit strengthens us for every good work and patience.

**Application:** Counselors should help counselees identify areas where fruit is lacking and guide them toward Spirit-filled living through prayer, obedience, and dependence on God's promises.

### 6. The Spirit Empowers the Word

The Spirit and the Word work together—never apart. The Spirit brings the Word alive in the heart.

- **Ephesians 6:17** – The Word of God is the "sword of the Spirit."
- **1 Corinthians 2:12–13** – We understand spiritual truths because of the Spirit.
- **Nehemiah 9:20** – God gave His Spirit to instruct His people.

**Application:** In counseling, Scripture must be central, but the Spirit must apply it. Counselors cannot rely only on Bible knowledge—they must prayerfully depend on the Spirit to illuminate truth in the counselee's heart.

### 7. The Spirit as Intercessor and Comforter

Often counselees are weak, weary, and unable to pray as they should. The Spirit steps in as an intercessor.

- **Romans 8:26–27** – The Spirit helps us in our weakness, interceding with groanings too deep for words.
- **John 14:27** – Jesus promises peace through the Spirit's presence.
- **Psalm 34:18** – Though not naming the Spirit directly, God by His Spirit is near to the brokenhearted.

**Application:** Counselors should encourage counselees that they are never alone—the Spirit Himself prays for them and comforts them in their darkest moments.

# THE PRINCIPLES OF NOUTHETIC COUNSELING

### 8. The Counselor's Dependence on the Spirit
The counselor, too, must walk by the Spirit. Human wisdom is powerless to change lives.

- **Zechariah 4:6** – "Not by might, nor by power, but by My Spirit, says the LORD."
- **1 Corinthians 2:4–5** – Paul relied not on persuasive words but on the Spirit's power.
- **Galatians 5:25** – Counselors must live and walk in the Spirit if they are to counsel in His strength.

**Application:** The counselor must be a Spirit-filled believer, relying daily on prayer, holiness, and submission to God's Word.

### Conclusion
The work of the Holy Spirit is indispensable to biblical counseling. He convicts of sin, gives new life, produces transformation, empowers the Word, intercedes for the weak, and bears fruit in the lives of believers.

Without Him, counseling is empty talk. With Him, counseling becomes a divine partnership, where the Spirit uses the Word and the counselor's faithfulness to bring lasting change.

### Reflection Questions for Chapter 6

1. How does John 14–16 describe the Spirit's role as Helper, Teacher, and Guide?
2. Why is conviction of sin (John 16:8) essential for true counseling?
3. How does the Spirit transform believers according to 2 Corinthians 3:18 and Galatians 5:16?
4. Why must counselors depend on both the Word and the Spirit?
5. How can the Spirit's intercession (Romans 8:26–27) comfort

struggling counselees?

# Chapter 7: Personal Responsibility in Change

**Introduction**

Biblical counseling recognizes the role of God's grace and the Spirit's power in transformation. Yet it also insists on **human responsibility**. A counselee cannot simply wait for change to happen automatically; he or she must **respond in obedience** to God's Word.

While modern psychology often casts people as helpless victims of circumstances, Scripture teaches that every person is morally responsible before God. Nouthetic Counseling calls counselees to take responsibility for their thoughts, words, and actions, and to pursue change through repentance and obedience.

**1. Each Person Is Accountable Before God**

God holds every individual personally responsible for sin and obedience.

- **Ezekiel 18:20** – "The soul who sins shall die. The son shall not bear the guilt of the father, nor the father bear the guilt of the son."
- **Romans 14:12** – "So then each of us shall give account of himself to God."
- **2 Corinthians 5:10** – We must all appear before Christ's judgment seat to give account for what we have done.

**Application in Counseling:** A counselee cannot blame parents, culture, or circumstances as excuses for sin. While others may influence us, each person is responsible for his or her own choices before God.

**2. Repentance Is the First Step in Change**

Real change begins with **repentance**—turning from sin to God.

- **Acts 3:19** – "Repent therefore and be converted, that your sins may be blotted out."
- **2 Corinthians 7:10** – Godly sorrow produces repentance leading to salvation.
- **Proverbs 28:13** – "He who covers his sins will not prosper, but whoever confesses and forsakes them will have mercy."

Repentance involves:

1. **Acknowledging sin** without excuse.
2. **Confessing sin** openly to God.
3. **Forsaking sin** with a determination to obey God's Word.

**Application:** Counselors must call counselees to repent specifically and personally, not vaguely or generally.

### 3. Obedience: Acting on God's Word

Hearing God's Word is not enough; the counselee must **do it**.

- **James 1:22–25** – Be doers of the Word, not hearers only, deceiving yourselves.
- **John 14:15** – Jesus: "If you love Me, keep My commandments."
- **Matthew 7:24–27** – The wise man builds on the rock by hearing and obeying Christ's words; the foolish man hears but does not obey.

**Application in Counseling:** Practical assignments (Bible study, journaling, reconciling relationships, replacing bad habits with godly ones) help counselees obey Scripture in daily life.

### 4. Taking Responsibility for Thoughts, Words, and Actions

Change requires responsibility in every area of life.

**a. Thoughts**

- Proverbs 23:7 – "As he thinks in his heart, so is he."
- 2 Corinthians 10:5 – Take every thought captive to obey Christ.
- Philippians 4:8 – Think on what is true, noble, just, pure, lovely, and praiseworthy.

### b. Words

- Matthew 12:36–37 – We will give account for every idle word.
- Proverbs 18:21 – Death and life are in the power of the tongue.
- Ephesians 4:29 – Speak only what builds up and gives grace.

### c. Actions

- Colossians 3:17 – Whatever you do, in word or deed, do all in the name of the Lord.
- 1 John 3:18 – Love in deed and truth, not only in word.
- Galatians 6:7–8 – We reap what we sow, whether to the flesh or the Spirit.

**Application:** The counselor must help the counselee identify specific sinful patterns in thought, word, and deed, and take responsibility to change by applying Scripture.

### 5. Avoiding the Victim Mentality

Many counselees blame others for their problems. But while circumstances can be difficult, they do not determine our obedience to God.

- **Genesis 3:12–13** – Adam blamed Eve; Eve blamed the serpent. Yet God held each accountable.
- **Philippians 2:14–15** – Believers are called to obey without

grumbling or disputing, even in hard situations.
- **1 Corinthians 10:13** – God always provides a way of escape from temptation; we cannot excuse sin as unavoidable.

**Application:** Counselors must lovingly challenge excuses and help counselees see their personal responsibility before God.

### 6. Personal Discipline and Effort
Change involves effort, empowered by grace.

- **1 Timothy 4:7** – "Discipline yourself for the purpose of godliness."
- **Philippians 2:12–13** – Work out your salvation with fear and trembling, for God works in you.
- **2 Peter 1:5–7** – Make every effort to add to your faith virtue, knowledge, self-control, perseverance, godliness, brotherly kindness, and love.

**Application:** Counselors can assign disciplines such as daily Bible reading, prayer, accountability relationships, Scripture memory, and journaling to help the counselee take responsibility for spiritual growth.

### 7. The Role of Accountability
Personal responsibility is strengthened through accountability within the church.

- **Hebrews 10:24–25** – We must encourage one another toward love and good works.
- **Ecclesiastes 4:9–10** – Two are better than one; if one falls, the other lifts him up.
- **Proverbs 27:17** – "As iron sharpens iron, so a man sharpens the countenance of his friend."

**Application:** A counselor may encourage the counselee to seek accountability partners, small group fellowship, or pastoral oversight for ongoing growth.

**Conclusion**

Personal responsibility in change is non-negotiable. God provides His Spirit and His Word, but He also commands His people to **repent, obey, and pursue holiness.** Counseling that excuses sin or leaves the counselee passive is not truly biblical.

The counselor's task is to lovingly, firmly call people to **own their sin, confess it, turn from it, and walk in new obedience.** By doing so, they demonstrate both the Spirit's power and their responsibility before God.

**Reflection Questions for Chapter 7**

1. What do Ezekiel 18:20 and Romans 14:12 teach about personal accountability?
2. Why is repentance the first step in change (Acts 3:19; Proverbs 28:13)?
3. How do James 1:22–25 and Matthew 7:24–27 highlight the necessity of obedience?
4. What areas of life (thoughts, words, actions) must a counselee take responsibility for?
5. How does accountability in the church strengthen personal responsibility for growth?

# Chapter 8: Hope in Christ as the Anchor of Counseling

**Introduction**

One of the most vital elements in biblical counseling is **hope.** Many who seek help feel trapped in despair, convinced their situation will never change. They may feel defeated by sin, weighed down by guilt, or overwhelmed by trials. Without hope, people give up.

But Scripture declares that **in Christ there is always hope.** Biblical counseling must continually hold out this hope—rooted not in circumstances, willpower, or human solutions, but in the promises of God and the finished work of Jesus Christ.

"This hope we have as an anchor of the soul, both sure and steadfast, and which enters the Presence behind the veil."
—Hebrews 6:19

**1. God Is the Source of Hope**

The Bible consistently points to God Himself as the fountain of all hope.

- **Romans 15:13** – "Now may the God of hope fill you with all joy and peace in believing, that you may abound in hope by the power of the Holy Spirit."
- **Psalm 39:7** – "And now, Lord, what do I wait for? My hope is in You."
- **Jeremiah 17:7** – "Blessed is the man who trusts in the LORD, and whose hope is the LORD."

**Application in Counseling:** The counselee must learn to shift hope away from self, others, or circumstances, and place it firmly in God.

**2. Hope Through the Promises of God's Word**

Hope grows as believers cling to God's promises.

- **Romans 15:4** – "Whatever things were written before were written for our learning, that we through the patience and comfort of the Scriptures might have hope."
- **Psalm 119:49–50** – "Remember the word to Your servant, upon which You have caused me to hope. This is my comfort in my affliction, for Your word has given me life."
- **2 Corinthians 1:20** – All the promises of God are "Yes" and "Amen" in Christ.

**Application:** Counselors must regularly bring counselees to God's promises—reminding them that God is faithful and His Word cannot fail.

### 3. Hope Rooted in the Resurrection of Christ

The resurrection of Jesus is the bedrock of Christian hope.

- **1 Peter 1:3** – "Blessed be the God and Father of our Lord Jesus Christ... who according to His abundant mercy has begotten us again to a living hope through the resurrection of Jesus Christ from the dead."
- **1 Corinthians 15:19–20** – If Christ is not risen, our hope is in vain; but because He lives, we have eternal hope.
- **John 11:25–26** – Jesus: "I am the resurrection and the life. He who believes in Me, though he may die, he shall live."

**Application in Counseling:** For the counselee facing despair, grief, or fear of death, the resurrection assures them that in Christ, nothing is final—not even death.

### 4. Hope in God's Faithfulness

Hope is anchored not in circumstances but in God's unchanging character.

- **Lamentations 3:21–23** – "This I recall to my mind, therefore I have hope: Through the LORD's mercies we are not consumed... His compassions fail not. They are new every morning; great is Your faithfulness."
- **Hebrews 10:23** – "Let us hold fast the confession of our hope without wavering, for He who promised is faithful."
- **Numbers 23:19** – God is not a man, that He should lie; He keeps His Word.

**Application:** The counselor reminds the counselee that even when feelings waver, God's faithfulness is sure.

## 5. Hope Sustains in Suffering

Scripture never promises a life free from trials. But it promises that hope in Christ sustains us in suffering.

- **Romans 5:3–5** – Tribulation produces perseverance, character, and hope—and this hope does not disappoint.
- **2 Corinthians 4:16–18** – Our present afflictions are light and momentary compared to the eternal weight of glory.
- **Psalm 42:5** – "Why are you cast down, O my soul? Hope in God, for I shall yet praise Him."

**Application in Counseling:** When counselees suffer, the counselor must lift their eyes to the eternal perspective, showing that trials are temporary, but hope in Christ is eternal.

## 6. Hope Anchored in the Gospel

At the core of counseling is the gospel—Christ's death and resurrection for sinners. This gospel gives unshakable hope.

- **Colossians 1:27** – "Christ in you, the hope of glory."
- **1 Timothy 1:1** – Jesus Christ is our hope.
- **Titus 2:11–13** – The grace of God trains us to live godly

lives while we wait for the blessed hope—the appearing of Christ.

**Application:** No matter the sin, failure, or despair, counselors must always bring counselees back to the gospel—Jesus is the source of lasting hope.

### 7. Hope and Perseverance
Hope strengthens perseverance in the Christian life.

- **Romans 8:24–25** – "We were saved in this hope, but hope that is seen is not hope... if we hope for what we do not see, we eagerly wait for it with perseverance."
- **Hebrews 12:1–2** – We run with endurance, looking unto Jesus, the author and finisher of our faith.
- **Philippians 1:6** – He who began a good work in us will complete it until the day of Christ.

**Application:** Counselors encourage counselees not to give up. Hope in Christ gives strength to endure temptation, hardship, and long struggles.

### 8. The Counselor as a Messenger of Hope
Counselors must constantly speak hope into the counselee's life.

- **Isaiah 50:4** – God gives the counselor "the tongue of the learned, that I should know how to speak a word in season to him who is weary."
- **1 Thessalonians 5:11** – "Therefore comfort each other and edify one another."
- **Hebrews 3:13** – Exhort one another daily so that none may be hardened by sin's deceitfulness.

**Application:** Every session must end not with despair but with encouragement from God's Word—assuring the counselee that in Christ, there is always hope.

## Conclusion

Hope is the anchor of biblical counseling. It rests in **God's character, God's promises, Christ's resurrection, and the gospel of grace.** Without hope, change is impossible; with hope, even the darkest situation can be transformed.

The counselor's calling is to lift the eyes of the counselee from their circumstances to the God of hope, filling them with confidence that His mercies are new every morning and His promises never fail.

### Reflection Questions for Chapter 8

1. Why is hope essential in biblical counseling (Hebrews 6:19)?
2. How do God's promises (Romans 15:4; Psalm 119:49–50) give hope in trials?
3. What role does the resurrection of Christ play in grounding our hope (1 Peter 1:3)?
4. How does God's faithfulness sustain hope even when circumstances seem hopeless (Lamentations 3:21–23)?
5. How can a counselor serve as a messenger of hope to those in despair (Isaiah 50:4)?

# Chapter 9: The Counselor's Life and Qualifications

**Introduction**

The effectiveness of biblical counseling depends not only on what is said but on **who the counselor is**. A counselor may know Scripture well, yet if his own life is inconsistent, his words lose credibility and power.

Nouthetic Counseling insists that those who counsel must live lives marked by **holiness, integrity, humility, and maturity in Christ**. Counselors are not perfect, but they must be examples of obedience and faith, pointing others not only with words but with their lives.

**1. Godly Character Is Essential**

The counselor's life must reflect the truth he proclaims.

- **1 Timothy 4:16** – "Take heed to yourself and to the doctrine. Continue in them, for in doing this you will save both yourself and those who hear you."
- **Philippians 3:17** – "Brethren, join in following my example, and note those who so walk, as you have us for a pattern."
- **1 Corinthians 11:1** – "Imitate me, just as I also imitate Christ."

**Application in Counseling:** The counselor must not only **teach truth** but also **model truth**. A life of hypocrisy destroys credibility, but a life of obedience strengthens the power of one's words.

**2. The Biblical Qualifications for Counselors**

While not every counselor is an elder or pastor, the qualifications for leadership in Scripture provide a model for those who minister to others.

- **1 Timothy 3:1–7** – Overseers must be above reproach, sober-minded, self-controlled, hospitable, able to teach, not greedy, gentle, and with a good reputation.
- **Titus 1:6–9** – Elders must hold firmly to the trustworthy Word, exhorting in sound doctrine and refuting error.
- **2 Timothy 2:24–25** – The Lord's servant must not quarrel but be gentle, patient, and able to teach.

**Application:** Counselors must strive to embody these traits, even if they are not in formal leadership.

### 3. Personal Holiness and Integrity

Counselors must walk in holiness, not perfection, but a consistent life of repentance and obedience.

- **1 Peter 1:15–16** – "As He who called you is holy, you also be holy in all your conduct."
- **Psalm 24:3–4** – Only those with clean hands and a pure heart can stand in God's presence.
- **Hebrews 12:14** – "Pursue peace with all people, and holiness, without which no one will see the Lord."

**Application:** The counselor who tolerates secret sin in his own life undermines the counseling process. Holiness builds trust and authority.

### 4. Dependence on God's Word

The counselor's wisdom must not come from human philosophy but from Scripture.

- **Colossians 3:16** – "Let the word of Christ dwell in you richly in all wisdom, teaching and admonishing one another."
- **Psalm 1:2–3** – The blessed man delights in God's law, meditating day and night, and prospers in his ways.

# THE PRINCIPLES OF NOUTHETIC COUNSELING 53

- **Joshua 1:8** – Meditating on the Word brings strength and success in God's eyes.

**Application:** A counselor must be a diligent student of the Word, applying it to his own life before applying it to others.

### 5. A Life of Prayer

Without prayer, counseling becomes human effort. The counselor must continually intercede for wisdom and for the counselee's transformation.

- **Colossians 4:2–4** – Continue earnestly in prayer, praying for open doors and clarity in speaking.
- **James 1:5** – If any lacks wisdom, ask of God, who gives generously.
- **Ephesians 6:18** – Pray always in the Spirit, for all the saints.

**Application:** Prayer must saturate counseling—from preparation, to the sessions, to follow-up. The counselor prays both with and for the counselee.

### 6. Humility and Gentleness

The counselor must be humble, never lording over others, but serving in love.

- **Philippians 2:3–4** – Esteem others better than yourself.
- **Galatians 6:1** – Restore the fallen in a spirit of gentleness.
- **2 Corinthians 1:24** – "Not that we have dominion over your faith, but are fellow workers for your joy."

**Application:** Counselors must not approach with arrogance but with compassion, remembering they too are sinners saved by grace.

### 7. Compassion for the Hurting

A biblical counselor must reflect the heart of Christ, who was moved with compassion for the broken.

- **Matthew 9:36** – Jesus saw the crowds and had compassion, for they were like sheep without a shepherd.
- **Isaiah 42:3** – A bruised reed He will not break, and a smoldering wick He will not quench.
- **Romans 12:15** – Rejoice with those who rejoice, weep with those who weep.

**Application:** Counselors must enter into the pain of their counselees with empathy, not dismissing struggles but bearing burdens in love (Galatians 6:2).

### 8. Self-Control and Emotional Stability

Counselors must be stable, not easily angered or swayed by emotions.

- **Proverbs 16:32** – He who rules his spirit is better than one who takes a city.
- **Titus 2:2** – Older men are to be sober, dignified, and self-controlled.
- **James 1:19–20** – Be quick to hear, slow to speak, slow to anger.

**Application:** A counselor who lacks control of his temper or emotions cannot lead others into self-control.

### 9. The Counselor's Testimony Before Others

A counselor's reputation matters, both inside and outside the church.

- **1 Timothy 3:7** – Leaders must have a good testimony among outsiders.
- **Matthew 5:16** – Let your light shine before others, that they may see your good works and glorify God.
- **Philippians 2:15** – Believers must shine as lights in a

crooked generation.

**Application:** The counselor's life is a living testimony. Integrity outside the counseling session is just as important as what is spoken inside it.

## Conclusion

The counselor's qualifications are not about degrees or psychological training but about **character, holiness, dependence on Scripture, prayer, humility, compassion, and integrity.**

A counselor who lives in obedience to God's Word becomes a powerful instrument in His hands. As Paul told Timothy, counselors must take heed to themselves and their teaching—because their lives either strengthen or weaken their counsel.

**Reflection Questions for Chapter 9**

1. Why is the counselor's personal holiness essential for effective counseling (1 Timothy 4:16)?
2. What do the qualifications for elders in 1 Timothy 3 and Titus 1 teach us about a counselor's character?
3. How does humility and gentleness shape the way a counselor approaches others (Galatians 6:1)?
4. Why must counselors be people of prayer and the Word (Colossians 3:16; James 1:5)?
5. How can a counselor's testimony outside the counseling room affect their ministry (1 Timothy 3:7)?

# Chapter 10: Listening and Discernment

**Introduction**

Effective counseling begins not with speaking, but with **listening**. Many rush to give advice, but biblical counselors must first understand. Scripture shows that wise listening requires patience, humility, and discernment. Counselors must learn to listen not only to words, but also to the heart behind the words, discerning motives, fears, and desires in light of God's Word.

"He who answers a matter before he hears it, it is folly and shame to him."
—Proverbs 18:13

Nouthetic counseling is not a one-sided lecture; it is Spirit-led dialogue that requires listening carefully and discerning biblically.

**1. The Call to Listen Carefully**

The Bible elevates the importance of listening before speaking.

- **James 1:19** – "Let every man be swift to hear, slow to speak, slow to wrath."
- **Proverbs 18:2** – "A fool has no delight in understanding, but in expressing his own heart."
- **Ecclesiastes 5:1-2** – Approach with reverence and humility, listening more than speaking.

**Application in Counseling:** Counselors must create a safe space where the counselee can open up. Rushing to speak may miss the heart of the issue.

**2. Listening to Understand the Heart**

Words often conceal deeper struggles. The counselor must listen beneath the surface.

- **Luke 6:45** – "Out of the abundance of the heart his mouth

speaks."
- **Proverbs 20:5** – "Counsel in the heart of man is like deep water, but a man of understanding will draw it out."
- **Jeremiah 17:9–10** – The heart is deceitful; God searches it and reveals motives.

**Application:** Listening well means asking questions that uncover what lies beneath the words—hidden fears, idols, or sins that must be addressed with Scripture.

### 3. Discernment: Testing What Is Heard

Not everything a counselee says is accurate. Counselors need discernment to test words against God's truth.

- **1 John 4:1** – "Test the spirits, whether they are of God."
- **Hebrews 5:14** – Mature believers have their senses trained to discern good and evil.
- **Proverbs 14:15** – "The simple believes every word, but the prudent considers well his steps."

**Application:** Counselors must gently challenge false beliefs, self-deception, or excuses by bringing Scripture into the conversation.

### 4. The Example of Christ as a Listener

Jesus was the Master Listener. He asked questions, drew people out, and listened with compassion.

- **Luke 24:17–19** – On the road to Emmaus, Jesus asked questions before teaching truth.
- **John 4:7–29** – With the Samaritan woman, Jesus listened, then exposed her heart with gentle yet firm words.
- **Mark 10:51** – Jesus asked the blind man, "What do you

want Me to do for you?"—though He already knew.

**Application:** Counselors should imitate Christ—listening attentively, asking wise questions, and then applying truth with precision.

### 5. Avoiding Common Pitfalls in Listening
Poor listening can harm counseling.

- **Interrupting** – Proverbs 18:13 warns against answering before hearing fully.
- **Judging motives prematurely** – Only God sees the heart (1 Samuel 16:7).
- **Surface listening** – Failing to ask deeper questions that uncover root issues.
- **Listening without Scripture** – Without God's truth, listening becomes mere empathy, not true counsel.

**Application:** Counselors must listen attentively but always move toward applying God's Word to the heart.

### 6. Asking Wise Questions
Proverbs commends the value of good questions.

- **Proverbs 20:5** – Drawing out counsel in the heart requires careful inquiry.
- **Proverbs 25:11** – "A word fitly spoken is like apples of gold in settings of silver."
- **Matthew 16:15** – Jesus asked, "But who do you say that I am?"—a heart-revealing question.

**Application:** Counselors should ask open-ended, thoughtful questions that help counselees reflect on their lives in light of God's truth.

## 7. Discernment by the Spirit

Discernment is not merely intellectual—it is Spirit-given.

- **1 Corinthians 2:12–15** – The Spirit reveals spiritual truths to those who are spiritual.
- **Philippians 1:9–10** – Paul prays that love may abound with knowledge and discernment, approving what is excellent.
- **Isaiah 11:2–3** – The Spirit of the Lord gives wisdom, understanding, counsel, and knowledge.

**Application:** Counselors must depend on the Holy Spirit for insight, asking Him to reveal hidden sins, fears, and lies that block transformation.

## 8. Listening with Compassion

True listening is more than collecting information—it is entering into the counselee's pain.

- **Romans 12:15** – "Rejoice with those who rejoice, and weep with those who weep."
- **Galatians 6:2** – Bear one another's burdens and so fulfill the law of Christ.
- **Hebrews 4:15** – Christ sympathizes with our weaknesses.

**Application:** Listening with compassion builds trust and communicates the heart of Christ.

### Conclusion

Biblical counseling requires more than speaking truth—it requires listening carefully, discerning wisely, and applying Scripture faithfully. Counselors must listen beyond the words to the heart, guided by the Spirit, asking wise questions, and responding with compassion and truth.

# THE PRINCIPLES OF NOUTHETIC COUNSELING

When listening and discernment are exercised together, the counselor becomes a skilled physician of the soul, applying the healing balm of God's Word to the deepest wounds.

**Reflection Questions for Chapter 10**

1. What does Proverbs 18:13 teach about the danger of speaking before listening?
2. How can a counselor listen not just to words but to the heart (Luke 6:45; Proverbs 20:5)?
3. Why is discernment necessary in counseling (Hebrews 5:14; 1 John 4:1)?
4. How does Jesus model compassionate listening (John 4; Luke 24:17–19)?
5. What role does the Holy Spirit play in giving discernment to the counselor (1 Corinthians 2:12–15)?

# Chapter 11: Speaking the Truth in Love

**Introduction**

One of the greatest challenges in counseling is balancing **truth and love**. Some are quick to speak truth but lack gentleness, leaving wounds without healing. Others show love but avoid truth, leaving sin unaddressed.

Biblical counseling insists on holding both together—**truth without compromise, love without harshness.** This balance reflects Christ Himself, who was "full of grace and truth" (John 1:14).

**1. The Biblical Command**

"But, speaking the truth in love, may grow up in all things into Him who is the head—Christ."

—Ephesians 4:15

This verse gives the counselor both the **method** (speaking truth in love) and the **goal** (spiritual maturity in Christ).

- **Truth** – God's Word, unchanging and authoritative (John 17:17).
- **Love** – Genuine concern for the counselee's good, reflecting Christ's heart (1 Corinthians 13:1–7).

**Application:** The counselor must not sacrifice one for the other. Truth without love becomes cruelty; love without truth becomes deception.

**2. The Example of Christ**

Jesus perfectly combined truth and love in His ministry.

- **John 1:14** – Jesus was full of grace and truth.
- **John 8:11** – To the adulterous woman: "Neither do I condemn you; go and sin no more." Truth confronted sin; grace offered forgiveness.

- **Mark 10:21** – To the rich young ruler: "Jesus, looking at him, loved him, and said to him..." Even hard truth came from love.
- **Revelation 3:19** – "As many as I love, I rebuke and chasten."

**Application:** Counselors must imitate Christ—speaking with compassion while refusing to compromise truth.

### 3. The Example of Paul

Paul's ministry also modeled this balance.

- **1 Thessalonians 2:7–8** – Paul cared like a nursing mother, sharing not only the gospel but his very life.
- **Acts 20:20–21** – He did not shrink from declaring what was profitable, preaching repentance and faith.
- **2 Corinthians 2:4** – Paul wrote "out of much affliction and anguish of heart, with many tears... that you might know the love which I have so abundantly for you."

**Application:** Truth must be delivered with tenderness, even when it is hard to hear.

### 4. The Role of Truth in Counseling

Truth is non-negotiable in counseling because only truth sets people free.

- **John 8:31–32** – "If you abide in My word... you shall know the truth, and the truth shall make you free."
- **Psalm 119:160** – "The entirety of Your word is truth."
- **Proverbs 12:19** – "The truthful lip shall be established forever."

# THE PRINCIPLES OF NOUTHETIC COUNSELING

**Application:** Counselors must never dilute or distort Scripture for fear of offending. Sin must be named, and God's standards must be upheld.

## 5. The Role of Love in Counseling

Truth must be delivered in love to bring healing.

- **1 Corinthians 13:1–2** – Without love, even the greatest truth-telling is worthless.
- **Colossians 3:12–14** – Counselors must clothe themselves with compassion, kindness, humility, gentleness, patience, and above all, love.
- **Proverbs 15:1** – "A soft answer turns away wrath, but a harsh word stirs up anger."

**Application:** The counselor's tone, body language, and manner must show care and gentleness, not pride or harshness.

## 6. Avoiding Two Extremes

Counselors often fall into one of two errors:

- **Truth without love** – Harsh, legalistic, condemning. This crushes instead of restores.
- **Love without truth** – Permissive, sentimental, compromising. This comforts but does not heal.

**Biblical balance:**

- **Galatians 6:1** – Restore in a spirit of gentleness, but still call sin "sin."
- **2 Timothy 4:2** – Preach the Word, rebuke and exhort, but with great patience.

**Application:** The counselor must prayerfully check motives: "Am I speaking to prove myself right, or to lovingly restore this person?"

### 7. Speaking with Wisdom and Grace

Truth must be communicated with wisdom, sensitivity, and grace.

- **Colossians 4:6** – "Let your speech always be with grace, seasoned with salt, that you may know how you ought to answer each one."
- **Proverbs 25:11** – "A word fitly spoken is like apples of gold in settings of silver."
- **Ecclesiastes 12:10** – "The Preacher sought to find acceptable words; and what was written was upright—words of truth."

**Application:** Timing and tone matter. The right truth at the wrong time or in the wrong way can hinder healing.

### 8. Love That Points to Repentance

Love does not mean avoiding confrontation; true love calls people to repentance.

- **2 Timothy 2:24–26** – The Lord's servant must correct opponents with gentleness, that God may grant them repentance.
- **Proverbs 27:6** – "Faithful are the wounds of a friend, but the kisses of an enemy are deceitful."
- **James 5:19–20** – Turning a sinner from his error saves his soul from death.

**Application:** Loving truth-telling may hurt at first, but it produces the fruit of repentance and life.

### 9. Speaking the Gospel

All truth in counseling must ultimately point to Christ.

- **Ephesians 4:21** – Truth is in Jesus.
- **John 14:6** – Jesus is the way, the truth, and the life.
- **Colossians 1:28** – Him we proclaim, warning and teaching in all wisdom, to present everyone mature in Christ.

**Application:** Counselors must not only expose sin but also point to the gospel—Christ's forgiveness, grace, and power to change.

**Conclusion**

Speaking the truth in love is the lifeblood of biblical counseling. Without truth, there is no freedom; without love, there is no healing. The counselor must prayerfully seek to embody both, imitating Christ who came full of grace and truth.

Truth confronts sin. Love restores the sinner. Together, they lead to transformation into Christlikeness.

**Reflection Questions for Chapter 11**

1. Why must truth and love always go together in counseling (Ephesians 4:15)?
2. How did Jesus model the perfect balance of grace and truth (John 8:11; Mark 10:21)?
3. Why is truth essential for freedom from sin (John 8:31–32)?
4. What dangers come from truth without love, or love without truth?
5. How can counselors wisely season their words with grace (Colossians 4:6)?

# Chapter 12: The Process of Change
# Put Off, Renew, Put On

**Introduction**

Biblical counseling teaches that true change is possible—not by willpower, self-help techniques, or positive thinking, but by following God's clear process of transformation. The apostle Paul outlines this process repeatedly:

1. **Put off** sinful behaviors, thoughts, and habits.
2. **Renew** the mind with God's truth.
3. **Put on** Christlike behaviors in obedience to the Word.

This threefold pattern, found in **Ephesians 4:22-24** and **Colossians 3:8-14**, gives a practical blueprint for lasting change.

**1. The Biblical Pattern of Change**

Paul describes the Christian life as a process of replacement:

"Put off, concerning your former conduct, the old man which grows corrupt according to the deceitful lusts, and be renewed in the spirit of your mind, and... put on the new man which was created according to God, in true righteousness and holiness."

—Ephesians 4:22-24

- **Put off** – Removing sinful patterns rooted in the flesh.
- **Renew** – Changing the way we think, believe, and desire by God's truth.
- **Put on** – Replacing old habits with new, righteous ones.

This is not behavior modification but **heart transformation.**

**2. Putting Off the Old Life**

The first step in change is **renouncing sinful patterns.**

- **Colossians 3:8-9** – "But now you must put off all these: anger, wrath, malice, blasphemy, filthy language out of your mouth."
- **Romans 13:12** – "Let us cast off the works of darkness, and let us put on the armor of light."
- **Hebrews 12:1** – Lay aside every weight and sin which so easily ensnares us.

**Application:** A counselee must identify specific sins—not just "I struggle," but "I must put off lying, anger, impurity, laziness, gossip, etc."

### 3. The Renewing of the Mind

The second step is to **change thinking** with God's truth.

- **Romans 12:2** – Transformation comes by renewing the mind.
- **Psalm 119:11** – "Your word I have hidden in my heart, that I might not sin against You."
- **John 17:17** – "Sanctify them by Your truth. Your word is truth."

**Application:** Counselors must help counselees replace lies with truth.

- "I can't change" → **Philippians 4:13** – "I can do all things through Christ."
- "God doesn't care" → **1 Peter 5:7** – He cares for you.
- "I must get revenge" → **Romans 12:19** – Vengeance belongs to God.

### 4. Putting On the New Life

The final step is replacing sin with righteousness.

- **Colossians 3:12–14** – Put on tender mercies, kindness, humility, meekness, longsuffering, forgiveness, and love.
- **Romans 13:14** – "Put on the Lord Jesus Christ, and make no provision for the flesh."
- **Galatians 5:22–23** – The fruit of the Spirit replaces the works of the flesh.

**Application:** True change is not just stopping sin, but practicing godly alternatives.

- Lying → Speak truth (Ephesians 4:25).
- Stealing → Work honestly and give (Ephesians 4:28).
- Corrupt speech → Words that edify (Ephesians 4:29).
- Bitterness → Forgiveness (Ephesians 4:31–32).

## 5. Case Examples
### a. Anger

- Put off: Rage, outbursts (Colossians 3:8).
- Renew: Recognize God's justice (Romans 12:19).
- Put on: Kindness, forgiveness (Ephesians 4:32).

### b. Anxiety

- Put off: Worry (Matthew 6:25).
- Renew: Trust in God's care (Philippians 4:19).
- Put on: Prayer and thanksgiving (Philippians 4:6–7).

### c. Lust

- Put off: Sexual immorality (1 Thessalonians 4:3–5).
- Renew: Remember your body is the temple of the Spirit (1 Corinthians 6:19–20).

- Put on: Purity, honoring God with your body (2 Timothy 2:22).

**d. Laziness**

- Put off: Slothfulness (Proverbs 24:30–34).
- Renew: Work as unto the Lord (Colossians 3:23).
- Put on: Diligence and faithfulness (Proverbs 13:4).

## 6. The Role of the Holy Spirit

This process is Spirit-empowered, not self-generated.

- **Philippians 2:13** – God works in us to will and do His pleasure.
- **Galatians 5:16** – Walk by the Spirit and you will not fulfill the lusts of the flesh.
- **2 Corinthians 3:18** – The Spirit transforms us into Christ's image.

**Application:** Counselors must encourage prayer, dependence, and walking in step with the Spirit.

## 7. Perseverance in the Process

Change is often gradual.

- **Philippians 1:6** – He who began a good work will complete it.
- **Hebrews 10:36** – You need endurance, to receive the promise.
- **Galatians 6:9** – Do not grow weary in doing good, for in due season you will reap.

# THE PRINCIPLES OF NOUTHETIC COUNSELING

**Application:** Counselors must encourage patience and perseverance, reminding counselees that setbacks are opportunities to repent and continue, not to quit.

## Conclusion

The process of change is clear: **Put off sin, renew the mind, put on righteousness.** It is Spirit-empowered, Word-driven, and Christ-centered.

Counseling that follows this pattern leads to real transformation, because it addresses both the root (the heart) and the fruit (behavior).

## Reflection Questions for Chapter 12

1. What does Ephesians 4:22–24 teach about the threefold process of change?
2. How does renewing the mind (Romans 12:2) differ from mere behavior modification?
3. Why is it important to replace sinful behavior with godly alternatives (Ephesians 4:25–32)?
4. How can counselors use case examples (anger, anxiety, lust, laziness) to illustrate the process?
5. How does the Holy Spirit empower change, and why must perseverance be emphasized?

# Chapter 13: Dealing with Anger

**Introduction**

Anger is one of the most common struggles counselees bring into the counseling room. Some explode in rage, others simmer in bitterness, while others justify their outbursts as "just the way I am." Yet Scripture teaches that anger, when uncontrolled or misdirected, leads to destruction.

Nouthetic counseling addresses anger not by suppressing it or excusing it, but by uncovering its sinful roots, exposing its consequences, and guiding the counselee to **put off sinful anger and put on Christlike responses.**

"So then, my beloved brethren, let every man be swift to hear, slow to speak, slow to wrath; for the wrath of man does not produce the righteousness of God."
—James 1:19–20

**1. Understanding Anger**

Anger itself is not always sinful. God expresses righteous anger against sin (Psalm 7:11; Romans 1:18). Jesus displayed holy anger in cleansing the temple (John 2:13–17; Mark 3:5).

But human anger is usually **self-centered, uncontrolled, and destructive.** The Bible warns against the sinful misuse of anger.

- **Proverbs 14:17** – "A quick-tempered man acts foolishly."
- **Ecclesiastes 7:9** – "Do not hasten in your spirit to be angry, for anger rests in the bosom of fools."
- **Proverbs 29:22** – "An angry man stirs up strife, and a furious man abounds in transgression."

**Application:** Counselors must help counselees distinguish between righteous anger (rooted in God's glory and justice) and sinful anger (rooted in selfishness, pride, or control).

## 2. The Causes of Sinful Anger

Anger often flows from deeper heart issues.

- **Pride** – Anger arises when our pride is wounded. (Proverbs 13:10)
- **Selfish desires** – "What causes quarrels and fights among you? Is it not your passions...?" (James 4:1–2).
- **Unmet expectations** – Jonah grew angry when God showed mercy (Jonah 4:1–4).
- **Fear or insecurity** – Saul's jealousy produced rage against David (1 Samuel 18:6–12).

**Application:** In counseling, the root must be addressed—not just the outward explosion but the inner idols of the heart.

## 3. The Consequences of Uncontrolled Anger

Scripture repeatedly warns of the dangers of sinful anger.

- **Proverbs 15:18** – A hot-tempered man stirs up strife.
- **Matthew 5:21–22** – Jesus equates unjust anger with the root of murder.
- **Ephesians 4:26–27** – Anger, when harbored, gives the devil a foothold.
- **Colossians 3:8** – Anger, wrath, and malice must be put away.

**Application:** The counselor should help counselees see that anger is not harmless—it destroys relationships, dishonors God, and opens doors for the enemy.

## 4. God's Command Regarding Anger

God's Word calls us to deal decisively with anger.

- **Ephesians 4:31–32** – "Let all bitterness, wrath, anger... be put away from you, and be kind... forgiving one another, even

# THE PRINCIPLES OF NOUTHETIC COUNSELING 77

as God in Christ forgave you."
- **Proverbs 16:32** – "He who is slow to anger is better than the mighty."
- **James 1:19–20** – Be slow to wrath, for human anger does not produce God's righteousness.

**Application:** Anger is not managed but **put off and replaced** with forgiveness, patience, and love.

### 5. Biblical Steps to Overcome Anger
#### a. Confess Sinful Anger

- **1 John 1:9** – If we confess our sins, He is faithful to forgive.
- **Proverbs 28:13** – Concealed sin hinders mercy; confession brings freedom.

#### b. Identify the Root

- **Psalm 139:23–24** – Ask God to search the heart and reveal sinful motives.
- **James 4:1–2** – Recognize selfish desires behind anger.

#### c. Renew the Mind

- **Romans 12:2** – Replace lies with truth.
- **Colossians 3:13** – Forgive as Christ forgave you.

#### d. Put On Godly Responses

- **Proverbs 15:1** – A soft answer turns away wrath.
- **Matthew 5:44** – Love your enemies, pray for those who persecute you.
- **Galatians 5:22–23** – Patience and self-control are fruits of the Spirit.

### 6. Case Example: Overcoming Anger in Marriage

A husband comes in saying, "My wife makes me so angry." The counselor must redirect:

- **Put off** blaming others (Genesis 3:12–13).
- **Renew** with truth: Anger flows from the heart (Luke 6:45).
- **Put on** patience, gentleness, and love (Colossians 3:12–14; 1 Corinthians 13:4–7).

Result: Change begins when the husband sees his responsibility before God and chooses Spirit-empowered responses.

### 7. Righteous Anger Directed by Love

Not all anger is sinful. Believers should share God's anger toward sin and injustice, but always in a way that honors Him.

- **Psalm 97:10** – "You who love the LORD, hate evil!"
- **Mark 3:5** – Jesus was angry at hardened hearts.
- **Ephesians 4:26** – "Be angry, and do not sin."

**Application:** Righteous anger is motivated by God's glory, expressed with self-control, and leads to constructive action—not revenge.

### 8. The Spirit's Power in Conquering Anger

Lasting victory comes not through human restraint but by the Holy Spirit.

- **Galatians 5:16** – Walk in the Spirit, and you will not fulfill the lusts of the flesh.
- **Romans 8:13** – By the Spirit we put to death the deeds of the body.
- **Philippians 4:13** – "I can do all things through Christ who strengthens me."

**Application:** Counselors must urge counselees to pray daily, yield to the Spirit, and seek accountability in their battle with anger.

## Conclusion

Anger is a destructive force when rooted in pride and selfishness, but through Christ it can be overcome. The process of change—putting off sinful anger, renewing the mind with God's truth, and putting on patience, forgiveness, and love—leads to freedom.

Anger does not have to dominate the believer's life. By God's grace, the counselee can learn to respond with self-control and compassion, reflecting the character of Christ.

### Reflection Questions for Chapter 13

1. What distinguishes righteous anger from sinful anger (Ephesians 4:26; Mark 3:5)?
2. According to James 4:1–2, what desires often fuel anger?
3. What are the consequences of harboring anger (Matthew 5:21–22; Ephesians 4:27)?
4. How can the "put off, renew, put on" model be applied to anger?
5. Why is the Holy Spirit essential in gaining victory over anger (Galatians 5:16)?

# Chapter 14: Overcoming Anxiety and Fear

**Introduction**

Anxiety and fear are among the most common struggles counselees face. Some live in constant worry about the future, others are paralyzed by fear of people, failure, or circumstances. Modern psychology often offers coping mechanisms or medication, but God's Word offers something far greater: **peace that surpasses understanding** (Philippians 4:7).

Biblical counseling does not deny the reality of anxiety but provides God's way of overcoming it—through trust in His promises, prayer, and dependence on His presence.

"Be anxious for nothing, but in everything by prayer and supplication, with thanksgiving, let your requests be made known to God; and the peace of God, which surpasses all understanding, will guard your hearts and minds through Christ Jesus."

—Philippians 4:6–7

**1. The Nature of Anxiety and Fear**

Anxiety is essentially **fear of the future**—worrying about what might happen. Fear can be healthy when it warns of danger, but sinful fear enslaves and controls the heart.

- **Proverbs 12:25** – "Anxiety in the heart of man causes depression, but a good word makes it glad."
- **Luke 12:25–26** – Worry cannot add a single hour to our lives.
- **2 Timothy 1:7** – "God has not given us a spirit of fear, but of power and of love and of a sound mind."

**Application:** Counselors must help counselees see that fear and anxiety flow from misplaced trust, focusing on circumstances rather than on God.

### 2. The Root Causes of Anxiety
Scripture identifies several roots of anxiety and fear:

- **Lack of trust in God** – Matthew 6:30, "O you of little faith."
- **Idolatry of control** – Wanting to control what belongs to God (James 4:13–15).
- **Fear of man** – Proverbs 29:25, "The fear of man brings a snare."
- **Unbelief in God's promises** – Hebrews 3:12 warns against an unbelieving heart.

**Application:** The counselor must move beyond symptoms to the heart, exposing where faith has been misplaced.

### 3. God's Commands Concerning Anxiety
God consistently commands His people not to be afraid but to trust Him.

- **Isaiah 41:10** – "Fear not, for I am with you; be not dismayed, for I am your God."
- **Joshua 1:9** – "Be strong and of good courage… for the LORD your God is with you wherever you go."
- **Matthew 6:25–34** – Jesus teaches not to worry about food, drink, or clothing, for the Father knows what we need.

**Application:** Anxiety is not simply an emotion—it is a faith issue. God commands us not to fear because He is trustworthy.

### 4. God's Provision for Peace
God promises peace in place of anxiety.

# THE PRINCIPLES OF NOUTHETIC COUNSELING

- **Philippians 4:6–7** – Prayer with thanksgiving brings God's peace.
- **John 14:27** – Jesus: "Peace I leave with you, My peace I give to you... let not your heart be troubled."
- **Isaiah 26:3** – "You will keep him in perfect peace, whose mind is stayed on You, because he trusts in You."

**Application:** Counselors should teach counselees to turn worry into prayer, replacing fearful thoughts with God's promises.

## 5. Practical Steps to Overcome Anxiety

### a. Pray Instead of Worry

- 1 Peter 5:7 – "Casting all your care upon Him, for He cares for you."
- Psalm 55:22 – "Cast your burden on the LORD, and He shall sustain you."

### b. Renew the Mind with Truth

- Matthew 6:33 – Seek first God's kingdom and righteousness.
- Romans 8:28 – All things work together for good for those who love God.
- Hebrews 13:5–6 – God will never leave nor forsake us.

### c. Focus on Today, Not Tomorrow

- Matthew 6:34 – "Do not worry about tomorrow, for tomorrow will worry about its own things."

### d. Practice Gratitude

- 1 Thessalonians 5:18 – Give thanks in everything.
- Colossians 3:15 – Let the peace of God rule in your hearts

and be thankful.

### e. Replace Fear with Faith

- Psalm 56:3–4 – "Whenever I am afraid, I will trust in You... What can flesh do to me?"
- Mark 4:40 – Jesus asked, "Why are you so fearful? How is it that you have no faith?"

### 6. Case Examples
### a. Fear of Finances

- Put off: Worry about money (Matthew 6:25).
- Renew: God provides for His children (Matthew 6:26; Philippians 4:19).
- Put on: Seek God's kingdom first (Matthew 6:33).

### b. Fear of People

- Put off: Fear of man (Proverbs 29:25).
- Renew: God is our helper (Hebrews 13:6).
- Put on: Boldness in Christ (Acts 4:19–20).

### c. Fear of the Future

- Put off: Worry about tomorrow (Matthew 6:34).
- Renew: God holds the future (Jeremiah 29:11).
- Put on: Trust in God's sovereignty (Proverbs 3:5–6).

### 7. The Spirit's Role in Conquering Fear
Victory over anxiety is not human effort but Spirit-empowered.

- **Romans 8:15** – We have received the Spirit of adoption, not of fear.

- **Galatians 5:22** – The Spirit produces peace as fruit.
- **2 Timothy 1:7** – The Spirit gives power, love, and a sound mind.

**Application:** The counselor must encourage the counselee to walk daily in the Spirit, relying on His power for peace.

### 8. Fixing Eyes on Christ
True peace is found only in Jesus.

- **Hebrews 12:2** – Look to Jesus, the author and finisher of our faith.
- **Matthew 14:30–31** – Peter sank when he looked at the storm but was safe when he fixed his eyes on Jesus.
- **Colossians 3:1–2** – Set your mind on things above, not on things on the earth.

**Application:** The counselor must consistently point anxious hearts to Christ, who is the Prince of Peace.

### Conclusion
Anxiety and fear lose their grip when the believer learns to trust God's character, rest in His promises, and walk in His presence. The process of change remains the same: **put off worry, renew the mind with God's Word, put on faith and peace.**

Biblical counseling offers real hope—not empty words, but the peace of Christ that guards the heart and mind.

### Reflection Questions for Chapter 14

1. What root causes of anxiety are identified in Matthew 6:25–34 and James 4:13–15?
2. How do God's promises in Philippians 4:6–7 and Isaiah 26:3 bring peace?
3. Why is prayer the biblical alternative to worry (1 Peter 5:7)?

4. How does the fear of man (Proverbs 29:25) differ from the fear of the Lord (Proverbs 14:27)?
5. What role does the Holy Spirit play in overcoming fear and anxiety (Romans 8:15; Galatians 5:22)?

# Chapter 15: Breaking Free from Addictions

**Introduction**

Addictions are among the most powerful chains that enslave people today. Whether it be drugs, alcohol, pornography, gambling, food, or even technology, addictions grip the heart, enslaving the mind and body. The world calls them "diseases" or "disorders," but Scripture calls them what they truly are: **bondage to sin and idolatry.**

Biblical counseling offers true hope, because in Christ, sinners can be set free.

"Therefore if the Son makes you free, you shall be free indeed."
—John 8:36

**1. The Nature of Addiction in Scripture**

Addictions are not merely physical habits—they are fundamentally **heart issues.** The Bible describes addiction as slavery.

- **Romans 6:16** – "Do you not know that to whom you present yourselves slaves to obey, you are that one's slaves whom you obey?"
- **Proverbs 5:22** – "His own iniquities entrap the wicked man, and he is caught in the cords of his sin."
- **Titus 3:3** – We were once "foolish, disobedient, deceived, serving various lusts and pleasures."

**Application:** The counselor must help the counselee see addiction not as a mere weakness but as slavery to sinful desires.

**2. The Root of Addiction: Idolatry**

At its core, addiction is **idolatry**—seeking satisfaction, comfort, or escape in something other than God.

- **Ezekiel 14:3** – Idols are set up in the heart.
- **Jeremiah 2:13** – God's people forsook Him, the fountain of living waters, and dug broken cisterns.
- **Philippians 3:19** – Some make their belly their god.

**Application:** Counselors must expose the idol behind the addiction. For example:

- Pornography may be rooted in lust and selfish pleasure.
- Alcohol may be rooted in a desire for escape.
- Gambling may be rooted in greed.

### 3. The Deceptive Nature of Addiction
Sin always promises pleasure but brings slavery and death.

- **Hebrews 11:25** – The pleasures of sin last only for a season.
- **James 1:14–15** – Desire gives birth to sin, and sin brings forth death.
- **Proverbs 23:29–35** – The drunkard seeks one more drink, though it brings sorrow, strife, and ruin.

**Application:** Counselors must help counselees see the lies of addiction and replace them with God's truth.

### 4. The Freedom Christ Provides
Addiction cannot be overcome by willpower, but by the power of Christ.

- **Romans 6:6–7** – Our old self was crucified with Christ, that we should no longer be slaves of sin.
- **2 Corinthians 5:17** – If anyone is in Christ, he is a new creation.
- **John 8:34–36** – "Whoever commits sin is a slave of sin...

# THE PRINCIPLES OF NOUTHETIC COUNSELING 89

therefore if the Son makes you free, you shall be free indeed."

**Application:** The counselor must emphasize union with Christ: freedom from sin's power is possible only through Him.

### 5. The Role of the Holy Spirit
Victory over addiction comes by walking in the Spirit.

- **Galatians 5:16** – "Walk in the Spirit, and you shall not fulfill the lust of the flesh."
- **Romans 8:13** – By the Spirit we put to death the deeds of the body.
- **1 Corinthians 10:13** – God provides a way of escape in every temptation.

**Application:** The counselor should encourage daily dependence on the Spirit, prayer, and Scripture memorization for strength in temptation.

### 6. The Process of Change: Put Off, Renew, Put On
#### a. Put Off

- Identify and confess addiction as sin (Proverbs 28:13; 1 John 1:9).
- Remove sources of temptation (Matthew 5:29–30).

#### b. Renew the Mind

- Replace lies ("I need this to cope") with truth ("Christ is sufficient") – Philippians 4:13, 19.
- Meditate on God's promises for strength (Psalm 119:11).

#### c. Put On

- Develop godly habits of worship, service, and fellowship

(Romans 12:1–2).
- Practice self-control as fruit of the Spirit (Galatians 5:23).
- Replace indulgence with purposeful living (Ephesians 5:15–18).

### 7. Accountability and the Body of Christ

Addictions thrive in secrecy. Healing requires accountability and fellowship.

- **James 5:16** – "Confess your trespasses to one another, and pray for one another, that you may be healed."
- **Hebrews 10:24–25** – Encourage one another daily, not neglecting to meet together.
- **Galatians 6:2** – Bear one another's burdens.

**Application:** Counselors must connect counselees to the local church for support, discipleship, and accountability.

### 8. Hope for the Addicted

There is always hope in Christ—no addiction is beyond His power.

- **1 Corinthians 6:9–11** – "Such were some of you. But you were washed, you were sanctified, you were justified in the name of the Lord Jesus."
- **Psalm 40:2** – God lifts us out of the pit and sets our feet on solid rock.
- **Micah 7:18–19** – God pardons iniquity and casts sins into the depths of the sea.

**Application:** Counselors must remind counselees of God's grace, offering both forgiveness and new strength in Christ.

### Conclusion

Addictions enslave, but Christ sets free. Biblical counseling does not merely offer coping strategies but calls people to repentance, faith, and transformation by the Spirit through God's Word.

The process is not easy, but it is possible. Through confession, repentance, renewal of the mind, Spirit-empowered obedience, and accountability in the body of Christ, the chains of addiction can be broken.

**Reflection Questions for Chapter 15**

1. How does Scripture describe addiction in terms of slavery (Romans 6:16; Proverbs 5:22)?
2. Why is idolatry at the heart of addiction (Jeremiah 2:13; Ezekiel 14:3)?
3. What does Christ's death and resurrection accomplish for those enslaved to sin (John 8:36; Romans 6:6–7)?
4. Why is accountability in the body of Christ essential for overcoming addiction (James 5:16)?
5. How can counselors bring both hope and responsibility to counselees struggling with addiction?

# Chapter 16: Marriage and Family Issues

**Introduction**

Marriage and family are God's design, the foundation of society, and a picture of Christ's relationship with His church (Ephesians 5:31–32). Yet they are also areas of great struggle. Many counselees come burdened with marital conflict, parenting difficulties, or family dysfunction.

The world often offers solutions rooted in psychology, compromise, or self-fulfillment. But biblical counseling restores hope by pointing families back to **God's design, God's roles, and God's power to heal broken relationships.**

**1. God's Design for Marriage**

Marriage is a covenant, not merely a contract.

- **Genesis 2:24** – "Therefore a man shall leave his father and mother and be joined to his wife, and they shall become one flesh."
- **Malachi 2:14–16** – God is a witness to the marriage covenant; He hates divorce.
- **Matthew 19:6** – "What God has joined together, let not man separate."

**Application:** Counselors must help couples see marriage not as disposable or negotiable, but as a lifelong covenant before God.

**2. The Roles of Husband and Wife**

God has given distinct but complementary roles.

**The Husband**

- Headship: **Ephesians 5:23** – "The husband is head of the wife, as also Christ is head of the church."
- Love: **Ephesians 5:25** – Husbands must love their wives as

Christ loved the church.
- Provision: **1 Timothy 5:8** – He must provide for his household.

## The Wife

- Helper: **Genesis 2:18** – God made woman as a helper fit for man.
- Submission: **Ephesians 5:22–24** – Wives are to submit to their husbands as to the Lord.
- Respect: **Ephesians 5:33** – She is to respect her husband.

**Application:** Counselors must carefully apply these truths with balance—never endorsing abuse, but affirming God's good order that leads to harmony.

### 3. Communication in Marriage

Many marital conflicts flow from sinful communication.

- **Proverbs 15:1** – A soft answer turns away wrath.
- **Ephesians 4:29** – Speak what builds up, not what tears down.
- **James 1:19** – Be quick to hear, slow to speak, slow to anger.

**Application:** Counselors should train couples to replace criticism, sarcasm, and silence with honest, gentle, and edifying communication.

### 4. Conflict Resolution

Conflict is inevitable, but Scripture provides a way to resolve it.

- **Colossians 3:13** – "Bear with one another, and forgive one another."
- **Matthew 18:15** – Address sin directly, not through gossip.
- **Ephesians 4:31–32** – Put away bitterness, anger, and malice;

# THE PRINCIPLES OF NOUTHETIC COUNSELING

replace with kindness and forgiveness.

**Application:** Couples must be taught to pursue reconciliation quickly (Ephesians 4:26), seeking peace rather than winning arguments.

### 5. The Role of Forgiveness
Unforgiveness destroys families. Forgiveness restores them.

- **Mark 11:25** – Forgive if you have anything against anyone.
- **Matthew 18:21–22** – Forgive "seventy times seven."
- **Colossians 3:13** – Forgive as Christ forgave you.

**Application:** Counselors must emphasize that forgiveness is not optional for believers.

### 6. Parenting in the Lord
Family counseling often involves children. God commands parents to raise their children in His ways.

- **Ephesians 6:4** – Fathers, do not provoke your children, but bring them up in the training and admonition of the Lord.
- **Deuteronomy 6:6–7** – Parents must teach God's Word diligently at home.
- **Proverbs 22:6** – Train up a child in the way he should go.

**Application:** Counselors must help parents see themselves as the primary disciplers of their children, modeling and teaching God's Word daily.

### 7. Children's Responsibility
Children also have a role in the family.

- **Ephesians 6:1–3** – "Children, obey your parents in the Lord, for this is right."
- **Colossians 3:20** – Pleasing the Lord through obedience.

- **Proverbs 1:8–9** – Listening to parental instruction brings wisdom.

**Application:** Counselors must encourage children and teens to honor God by honoring parents.

### 8. The Family as a Witness

A godly family is a powerful testimony to the world.

- **Joshua 24:15** – "As for me and my house, we will serve the LORD."
- **1 Timothy 3:4–5** – A leader must manage his household well.
- **Matthew 5:16** – Families are to shine as lights for God's glory.

**Application:** Counselors must lift the counselee's vision beyond personal happiness to see the family's role in God's mission.

### 9. Dealing with Family Brokenness

Some families come to counseling already deeply broken. Scripture still offers hope.

- **Psalm 34:18** – God is near to the brokenhearted.
- **Joel 2:25** – God restores the years the locusts have eaten.
- **2 Corinthians 5:17** – In Christ, brokenness can be made new.

**Application:** Counselors must remind counselees that no family is beyond God's power to restore.

### Conclusion

Marriage and family counseling must be firmly rooted in God's Word. The counselor points couples and parents back to God's design, guiding them to embrace their roles, communicate in love, resolve conflict biblically, forgive freely, and disciple their children faithfully.

A family that follows God's order becomes not only a place of peace and love but also a powerful witness of Christ's love to the world.

**Reflection Questions for Chapter 16**

1. What does Genesis 2:24 teach about the covenant nature of marriage?
2. What are the biblical roles of husbands and wives (Ephesians 5:22–33)?
3. How does Scripture guide conflict resolution in marriage (Matthew 18:15; Ephesians 4:31–32)?
4. What is the responsibility of parents toward their children (Deuteronomy 6:6–7; Ephesians 6:4)?
5. How can the family serve as a witness to the world (Joshua 24:15; Matthew 5:16)?

# Chapter 17: Depression and Despair

**Introduction**

Depression and despair are heavy burdens many counselees bring to the counseling room. They may feel hopeless, joyless, and overwhelmed by guilt, grief, or life's pressures. While the world often views depression as merely a medical condition, Scripture reveals that despair is deeply tied to the **heart, hope, and faith.**

Biblical counseling does not deny physical factors, but it emphasizes the spiritual battle at the core of depression. God's Word offers hope, comfort, and renewal for the downcast soul.

"Why are you cast down, O my soul? And why are you disquieted within me? Hope in God; for I shall yet praise Him, the help of my countenance and my God."
—Psalm 42:11

**1. The Reality of Depression in Scripture**

The Bible acknowledges the reality of deep discouragement and despair.

- **Elijah** – After his victory at Mount Carmel, Elijah fled in fear and wished for death (1 Kings 19:4).
- **David** – He often cried out in anguish: "My soul clings to the dust; revive me according to Your word" (Psalm 119:25).
- **Job** – He lamented bitterly in his suffering: "I loathe my life; I will give free course to my complaint" (Job 10:1).
- **Jeremiah** – Known as the "weeping prophet" (Jeremiah 20:14–18).

**Application:** Counselors must not dismiss or minimize the struggles of the downcast. Even godly saints experienced despair.

**2. Common Causes of Depression**

Scripture points to several possible sources:

- **Unconfessed sin** – Guilt weighs heavy (Psalm 32:3–4).
- **Loss or grief** – David mourned deeply for his child (2 Samuel 12:16–17).
- **Unmet expectations** – Elijah expected revival, but instead faced rejection (1 Kings 19).
- **Fear or anxiety** – Fear magnifies despair (Psalm 55:4–5).
- **Weariness** – Physical and emotional exhaustion (Galatians 6:9).
- **Hopelessness** – Forgetting God's promises (Lamentations 3:18–20).

**Application:** Counselors must discern the root causes—sometimes sin, sometimes suffering, sometimes both.

### 3. The Dangers of Despair
If left unchecked, despair can lead to:

- **Isolation** – Elijah withdrew from others (1 Kings 19:3–4).
- **Loss of perspective** – Jonah wanted death rather than obedience (Jonah 4:3).
- **Giving up on God's purposes** – Psalm 77:7–9 records doubts of God's goodness.
- **Even suicidal thoughts** – Though Scripture condemns self-destruction, several biblical figures wished for death.

**Application:** Counselors must take despair seriously, addressing hopeless thoughts with urgency and compassion.

### 4. God's Comfort for the Downcast
God meets the depressed with compassion and truth.

- **Psalm 34:18** – "The LORD is near to those who have a

broken heart."

- **2 Corinthians 1:3-4** – God comforts us in all tribulation so we may comfort others.
- **Isaiah 61:1-3** – Christ came to heal the brokenhearted and give the garment of praise for the spirit of heaviness.

**Application:** The counselor must bring the counselee back to God's presence, promises, and compassion.

### 5. Renewing Hope Through God's Word

The primary weapon against despair is hope in God's Word.

- **Psalm 119:50** – "This is my comfort in my affliction, for Your word has given me life."
- **Romans 15:4** – The Scriptures provide encouragement and hope.
- **Lamentations 3:21-23** – God's mercies are new every morning; great is His faithfulness.

**Application:** Counselors should assign daily Scripture meditation, focusing on God's promises of love, forgiveness, and presence.

### 6. The Role of Prayer and Worship

Depression often silences prayer, but prayer revives the soul.

- **Philippians 4:6-7** – Prayer with thanksgiving brings peace.
- **Psalm 62:8** – Pour out your heart before God.
- **Acts 16:25** – Paul and Silas sang hymns in prison, lifting their spirits and testifying of God.

**Application:** Counselors should encourage counselees to pray honestly, even in weakness, and to worship as a weapon against despair.

### 7. The Importance of Fellowship

Isolation deepens despair, but fellowship brings encouragement.

- **Ecclesiastes 4:9–10** – Two are better than one; if one falls, the other lifts him up.
- **Hebrews 10:24–25** – Do not neglect assembling together, but encourage one another.
- **Galatians 6:2** – Bear one another's burdens.

**Application:** Counselors should urge counselees to seek Christian community, accountability, and encouragement.

### 8. Putting Off Despair and Putting On Hope
Using the biblical process of change:

- **Put off** hopeless thoughts: "I am abandoned" (Psalm 77:7–9).
- **Renew** the mind: God's promises never fail (Hebrews 13:5).
- **Put on** faith and praise: "I will yet praise Him, my Savior and my God" (Psalm 42:11).

**Application:** Encourage journaling, replacing lies with truth, and daily thanksgiving lists.

### 9. The Counselor's Role
Counselors must:

- Listen with compassion (Romans 12:15).
- Speak truth with gentleness (Ephesians 4:15).
- Pray faithfully for the counselee (Colossians 1:9–11).
- Continually point the downcast to Christ, the Man of Sorrows who understands their pain (Isaiah 53:3–4).

# THE PRINCIPLES OF NOUTHETIC COUNSELING

## Conclusion

Depression and despair are real, but they are not final. God's Word brings light into darkness, hope into despair, and joy into mourning. Through prayer, Scripture, fellowship, and renewed trust in God's promises, the downcast can find strength and restoration.

Christ is the ultimate answer for despair—He bore our griefs, carried our sorrows, and offers everlasting hope.

## Reflection Questions for Chapter 17

1. What biblical examples show that even godly people experienced despair (Elijah, David, Job, Jeremiah)?
2. How does unconfessed sin contribute to depression (Psalm 32:3-4)?
3. What promises of God bring comfort to the downcast (Psalm 34:18; Lamentations 3:21-23)?
4. How can prayer, worship, and fellowship help a believer overcome despair?
5. How does Isaiah 53:3-4 comfort those in depression by pointing to Christ?

# Chapter 18: Forgiveness and Reconciliation

**Introduction**

Few issues are as destructive in the counseling setting as **unforgiveness**. Bitterness poisons the heart, fractures relationships, and blocks spiritual growth. Many counselees carry heavy burdens because they refuse to forgive or because they long for reconciliation that seems impossible.

Forgiveness is not a suggestion but a command rooted in the gospel. Just as God forgave us in Christ, we must forgive others. True reconciliation is the fruit of forgiveness applied in relationships.

"And be kind to one another, tenderhearted, forgiving one another, even as God in Christ forgave you."
—Ephesians 4:32

**1. God's Forgiveness as the Foundation**

Our ability to forgive flows from God's forgiveness toward us.

- **Colossians 3:13** – Forgive one another as Christ forgave you.
- **Matthew 18:21–35** – The parable of the unforgiving servant shows the hypocrisy of receiving great mercy but refusing to show it.
- **Psalm 103:10–12** – God does not deal with us according to our sins but removes them as far as the east is from the west.

**Application:** Counselors must remind counselees that forgiveness is rooted in the gospel. We forgive because we have been forgiven.

**2. What Forgiveness Is**

Biblical forgiveness is not ignoring sin or excusing wrong. It is a **deliberate act of grace**:

- Releasing the offender from personal vengeance (Romans 12:19).
- Refusing to dwell on the offense (Isaiah 43:25).
- Choosing to pursue love and peace (Proverbs 10:12; Romans 12:18).

**Application:** Forgiveness is not a feeling but a choice of obedience, empowered by God's Spirit.

## 3. What Forgiveness Is Not

Forgiveness does not mean:

- Pretending sin didn't happen.
- Removing all consequences (Numbers 14:20–23).
- Immediate trust without evidence of change.
- Reconciliation without repentance (Luke 17:3).

**Application:** Counselors must clarify the difference between forgiveness (one-sided, heart release) and reconciliation (two-sided, relationship restoration).

## 4. The Dangers of Unforgiveness

Bitterness destroys the soul.

- **Hebrews 12:15** – A root of bitterness causes trouble and defiles many.
- **Matthew 6:14–15** – If we refuse to forgive, we cannot expect God's forgiveness in fellowship.
- **Proverbs 14:30** – Envy and bitterness rot the bones.

**Application:** Counselors must show counselees that unforgiveness enslaves them more than the offender.

## 5. God's Commands to Forgive

Forgiveness is non-negotiable for believers.

- **Mark 11:25** – Forgive whenever you stand praying.
- **Luke 17:3–4** – Even if a brother sins seven times in a day and repents, forgive him.
- **Romans 12:21** – Overcome evil with good.

**Application:** Forgiveness is not optional—it is obedience to Christ.

### 6. The Process of Forgiveness

**a. Acknowledge the Offense**

Do not minimize sin; call it what it is (Genesis 50:20).

**b. Release Vengeance**

Leave justice to God (Romans 12:19).

**c. Remember God's Forgiveness**

Reflect on the cross (Ephesians 4:32).

**d. Act in Love**

Pray for the offender (Matthew 5:44). Seek peace when possible (Romans 12:18).

### 7. Reconciliation: Forgiveness Applied

Forgiveness opens the door to reconciliation, though reconciliation requires repentance and restoration.

- **Matthew 5:23–24** – Be reconciled to your brother before offering worship.
- **2 Corinthians 5:18–19** – God reconciled us to Himself through Christ and gave us the ministry of reconciliation.
- **Romans 12:18** – Live peaceably with all, as much as depends on you.

**Application:** Counselors must help counselees pursue reconciliation when possible, but also rest in peace if the other party refuses.

### 8. Case Example: Bitterness in Marriage

A wife holds bitterness against her husband for years of neglect. The counselor must:

- Help her see God's command to forgive.
- Guide her to release vengeance and bitterness.
- Encourage steps toward reconciliation if repentance occurs.
- Remind her that forgiveness honors Christ, even if full reconciliation takes time.

### 9. The Power of the Gospel

The gospel is the ultimate model and motivation for forgiveness.

- **Romans 5:8** – Christ died for us while we were still sinners.
- **Luke 23:34** – Jesus prayed, "Father, forgive them," even as He was crucified.
- **Micah 7:18–19** – God delights in mercy, pardoning iniquity.

**Application:** Counselors must always point counselees to the cross as the example and power for forgiving others.

### Conclusion

Forgiveness is not easy, but it is essential. Refusing to forgive breeds bitterness, but granting forgiveness brings freedom and peace. Reconciliation, when possible, displays the power of the gospel to the world.

The counselor's task is to lead counselees to embrace forgiveness, release bitterness, and pursue peace, all in light of Christ's forgiveness of us.

**Reflection Questions for Chapter 18**

1. How does God's forgiveness in Christ form the basis for forgiving others (Colossians 3:13)?
2. What is the difference between forgiveness and reconciliation?
3. What dangers does unforgiveness bring (Hebrews 12:15; Matthew 6:14–15)?
4. How does the gospel empower forgiveness (Romans 5:8; Luke 23:34)?
5. How can a counselor guide someone stuck in bitterness toward true forgiveness?

# Chapter 19: Counseling Through Grief and Loss

**Introduction**

Grief and loss are universal experiences. Whether through death, illness, betrayal, or broken dreams, everyone encounters seasons of sorrow. Many counselees come burdened by grief that feels overwhelming.

The world often offers shallow comfort, distracting people from pain or teaching them to "move on." But biblical counseling offers something deeper: **God's presence, His promises, and the hope of eternal life.**

"The LORD is near to those who have a broken heart, and saves such as have a contrite spirit."
—Psalm 34:18

**1. The Reality of Grief**

Grief is not a sign of weakness but a natural response to loss. Scripture shows godly people grieving deeply.

- **Abraham** – Wept for Sarah (Genesis 23:2).
- **David** – Mourned Jonathan and Saul (2 Samuel 1:11–12).
- **Job** – Tore his robe and fell to the ground in grief (Job 1:20).
- **Jesus** – Wept at Lazarus' tomb (John 11:35).

**Application:** Counselors must validate grief as a real and appropriate response, not something to be rushed or denied.

**2. Causes of Grief**

Grief may arise from:

- **Death of a loved one** – John 11.
- **Broken relationships** – Psalm 55:12–14.

- **Personal failure or sin** – Psalm 51.
- **Loss of health, security, or dreams** – Job 1–2.

**Application:** Identifying the source of grief helps direct the counselee to God's specific comfort.

## 3. The Dangers in Grief

While grief is natural, it can lead to despair if not brought to God.

- **Isolation** – Psalm 102:7 describes loneliness.
- **Bitterness** – Naomi became "Mara" (Ruth 1:20).
- **Hopelessness** – Lamentations 3:18, "My hope has perished."
- **Turning away from God** – Job's wife urged him to "curse God and die" (Job 2:9).

**Application:** Counselors must lovingly warn against sinful responses to grief and point counselees back to God.

## 4. God's Comfort in Grief

God meets His children in sorrow with His comfort.

- **2 Corinthians 1:3–4** – God is the "Father of mercies and God of all comfort."
- **Psalm 23:4** – Even in the valley of the shadow of death, God is with us.
- **Isaiah 41:10** – God promises His presence, strength, and help.

**Application:** Counselors should remind counselees that God does not abandon them in grief; He draws near.

## 5. The Hope of Eternal Life

The greatest comfort for Christians is the hope of resurrection.

# THE PRINCIPLES OF NOUTHETIC COUNSELING 113

- **1 Thessalonians 4:13-14** – We do not grieve as those without hope.
- **John 14:1-3** – Jesus prepares a place for His people.
- **Revelation 21:4** – God will wipe away every tear; no more death or sorrow.

**Application:** Counselors must continually point grieving believers to the eternal perspective: death is not the end.

### 6. Practical Steps for Walking Through Grief
#### a. Lament Honestly Before God

- Psalm 62:8 – Pour out your heart before Him.
- Lamentations 2:19 – Cry out to the Lord in distress.

#### b. Remember God's Promises

- Romans 8:38-39 – Nothing separates us from God's love.
- Hebrews 13:5 – God will never leave nor forsake us.

#### c. Pray and Worship

- Psalm 42:5 – "Hope in God, for I shall yet praise Him."
- Habakkuk 3:17-18 – Rejoice in the Lord even in loss.

#### d. Lean on Christian Community

- Galatians 6:2 – Bear one another's burdens.
- Romans 12:15 – Weep with those who weep.

#### e. Serve and Comfort Others

- 2 Corinthians 1:4 – Comfort others with the comfort you have received.

### 7. Case Example: Grieving Widow

A widow struggles after the death of her husband. The counselor must:

- Validate her grief, reminding her it is natural and not sinful.
- Point her to God's nearness (Psalm 34:18).
- Remind her of the hope of resurrection (1 Thessalonians 4:13–14).
- Encourage her to lean on the church for support and to serve others as she heals.

### 8. Christ the Man of Sorrows

The ultimate comfort in grief is Christ Himself.

- **Isaiah 53:3–4** – Jesus was a Man of sorrows, acquainted with grief.
- **Hebrews 4:15** – He sympathizes with our weaknesses.
- **Matthew 11:28** – He invites the weary and burdened to find rest in Him.

**Application:** Counselors must direct the grieving counselee to Christ, who knows their pain and offers Himself as their refuge.

### Conclusion

Grief is real, but it is not hopeless. God comforts the brokenhearted, His promises sustain His children, and eternal life in Christ gives lasting hope. Biblical counseling does not minimize pain but points counselees to the One who turns mourning into joy.

"Weeping may endure for a night, but joy comes in the morning."
—Psalm 30:5

## Reflection Questions for Chapter 19

1. How does the Bible show that even godly people experienced grief (Abraham, David, Job, Jesus)?
2. What dangers can grief lead to if not brought to God (bitterness, hopelessness, isolation)?
3. How do passages like 2 Corinthians 1:3–4 and Psalm 23:4 describe God's comfort?
4. What is the Christian hope in grief according to 1 Thessalonians 4:13–14 and Revelation 21:4?
5. How does Christ as the Man of Sorrows (Isaiah 53:3–4) bring comfort to the grieving?

# Chapter 20: Counseling the Church Body

**Introduction**

Biblical counseling is not limited to a private office—it is the responsibility of the **whole church**. The church is not merely a gathering place for worship but a living body where believers are called to **bear one another's burdens, exhort one another, and encourage one another daily**.

Every member of Christ's body has a role in soul care. Counseling in the church is about cultivating a culture of discipleship, accountability, and love, where God's people are instruments of His grace in one another's lives.

"Now you are the body of Christ, and members individually."
—1 Corinthians 12:27

**1. The Church's Role in Counseling**

God never intended the Christian life to be lived in isolation.

- **Hebrews 10:24-25** – Stir up one another to love and good works, not forsaking assembling together.
- **Romans 15:14** – Believers are full of goodness, filled with knowledge, and able to admonish one another.
- **Galatians 6:2** – Bear one another's burdens, and so fulfill the law of Christ.

**Application:** Counseling is not just for pastors—it is the calling of every believer to speak truth in love within the body.

**2. Mutual Accountability**

Accountability strengthens growth and helps prevent sin.

- **Hebrews 3:13** – Exhort one another daily, lest any be

hardened by the deceitfulness of sin.
- **Proverbs 27:17** – Iron sharpens iron, so one man sharpens another.
- **James 5:16** – Confess sins to one another and pray for one another.

**Application:** Counselors should encourage counselees to be connected in fellowship where accountability relationships can flourish.

### 3. The Ministry of Encouragement

Encouragement is a vital form of counseling within the church.

- **1 Thessalonians 5:11** – Encourage one another and build each other up.
- **Hebrews 12:12** – Strengthen weak hands and feeble knees.
- **Isaiah 35:3–4** – Speak courage to the fearful: "Be strong, do not fear!"

**Application:** Churches should be communities where words of life and encouragement are the norm, not criticism and gossip.

### 4. Equipping the Saints for Counseling

Pastors and leaders are called to equip believers to minister to one another.

- **Ephesians 4:11–12** – Christ gave pastors and teachers to equip the saints for the work of ministry.
- **Colossians 3:16** – Let the Word dwell richly among you, teaching and admonishing one another.
- **2 Timothy 2:2** – Train faithful men who will be able to teach others also.

**Application:** A biblical counseling church trains its members in Scripture, discipleship, and the ability to apply God's truth to life's struggles.

### 5. The Importance of Church Discipline

Sometimes counseling involves loving confrontation of sin through church discipline.

- **Matthew 18:15–17** – Address sin privately, then with witnesses, and finally before the church if unrepented.
- **1 Corinthians 5:1–5** – Discipline in the church protects purity and calls sinners to repentance.
- **2 Thessalonians 3:14–15** – Do not treat the disobedient as enemies but admonish them as brothers.

**Application:** Discipline is not about punishment but restoration, protecting the flock and calling the sinner back.

### 6. The Power of Corporate Prayer

The church counsels and strengthens one another through prayer.

- **Acts 2:42** – The early church devoted themselves to prayer together.
- **Acts 12:5** – The church prayed fervently for Peter in prison.
- **Philippians 4:6–7** – Prayer brings peace that guards the heart.

**Application:** Churches should pray regularly for one another's struggles, bearing each other's burdens before the Lord.

### 7. The Church as a Healing Community

The church is designed to be a place of refuge and healing.

- **James 1:27** – Care for orphans and widows in their distress.
- **Romans 12:15** – Rejoice with those who rejoice, weep with

those who weep.
- **Isaiah 61:1** – The gospel proclaims liberty to captives and healing for the brokenhearted.

**Application:** Churches must cultivate a culture of compassion, where broken people find grace, love, and hope in Christ.

### 8. Case Example: Restoring a Fallen Member

A man caught in adultery repents and seeks restoration. The church must:

- Apply discipline if necessary (1 Corinthians 5).
- Extend forgiveness upon repentance (2 Corinthians 2:6–8).
- Restore him gently (Galatians 6:1).
- Encourage him to walk in accountability and discipleship.

### 9. Christ the Head of the Church

All counseling in the church must flow from Christ, the Head.

- **Ephesians 1:22–23** – Christ is head over all things for the church.
- **Colossians 1:18** – He is the head of the body, the church.
- **John 15:5** – Apart from Christ we can do nothing.

**Application:** Counseling in the church is not about man's wisdom but Christ's authority and power working through His body.

### Conclusion

The church is God's ordained community for soul care. Counseling is not merely the job of a few but the ministry of the many—every member speaking truth in love, bearing burdens, offering encouragement, and pointing one another to Christ.

When the church lives out its calling, it becomes a place of healing, holiness, and hope, shining as a light to the world.

## Reflection Questions for Chapter 20

1. How does Romans 15:14 show that all believers are called to admonish one another?
2. What role does accountability play in counseling within the church (Hebrews 3:13; James 5:16)?
3. Why is encouragement such a vital ministry in the body of Christ (1 Thessalonians 5:11)?
4. How does church discipline serve the purpose of restoration (Matthew 18:15–17; 2 Thessalonians 3:14–15)?
5. In what ways can your church become more of a healing community (Romans 12:15; James 1:27)?

# Chapter 21: Counseling in Times of Crisis

**Introduction**

Crises often come suddenly—serious illness, tragic accidents, natural disasters, violence, or sudden loss. In such moments, counselees may feel overwhelmed, paralyzed, and unable to think clearly. Crisis counseling is not about offering quick fixes but about **bringing the presence, promises, and peace of God into moments of chaos.**

"God is our refuge and strength, a very present help in trouble. Therefore we will not fear."
—Psalm 46:1–2

**1. The Nature of a Crisis**

A crisis is a time of intense difficulty when normal coping mechanisms fail. In Scripture, we see many crises:

- **Job's losses** (Job 1–2).
- **David fleeing Saul** (1 Samuel 21–24).
- **The disciples in the storm** (Mark 4:35–41).
- **Paul shipwrecked and beaten** (Acts 27; 2 Corinthians 11:25–28).

**Application:** Counselors must recognize that crises are both trials and opportunities for God to show His power.

**2. Common Reactions to Crisis**

People may respond in sinful or godly ways:

- **Fear and panic** – Like the disciples crying, "Teacher, do You not care?" (Mark 4:38).
- **Anger and blame** – Job's wife told him to curse God (Job 2:9).

- **Hopelessness** – Elijah wished for death (1 Kings 19:4).
- **Faith and prayer** – Jehoshaphat sought God in crisis (2 Chronicles 20:3–4).

**Application:** Counselors must guide counselees to respond with faith instead of fear.

### 3. God's Promises in Crisis
God's Word assures His people of His presence and help.

- **Isaiah 41:10** – "Fear not, for I am with you; be not dismayed, for I am your God."
- **Psalm 34:17–19** – The Lord delivers the righteous out of all their troubles.
- **Romans 8:28** – All things work together for good for those who love God.
- **2 Corinthians 1:8–10** – God delivers us from deadly peril, and we set our hope on Him.

**Application:** Counselors must remind counselees that God is sovereign, faithful, and good—even in chaos.

### 4. Practical Steps for Crisis Counseling
#### a. Provide Presence and Compassion

- Romans 12:15 – Weep with those who weep.
- Job 2:13 – Job's friends initially sat silently with him.
- Galatians 6:2 – Bear one another's burdens.

#### b. Direct to Prayer and God's Word

- Philippians 4:6–7 – Prayer brings peace in turmoil.
- Psalm 119:50 – God's Word brings life and comfort.
- Matthew 11:28 – Christ invites the weary to find rest in Him.

# THE PRINCIPLES OF NOUTHETIC COUNSELING    125

### c. Help with Immediate Needs

- James 2:15–16 – Meeting physical needs is part of love.
- Acts 11:27–30 – The church provided relief in famine.

### d. Encourage Faith, Not Fear

- John 14:27 – Jesus gives peace, not as the world gives.
- Mark 5:36 – "Do not be afraid; only believe."
- 2 Timothy 1:7 – God gives a spirit of power, love, and a sound mind.

## 5. The Opportunity in Crisis
Crisis can lead to spiritual growth and turning to God.

- **Psalm 119:71** – "It is good for me that I have been afflicted, that I may learn Your statutes."
- **Romans 5:3–5** – Tribulation produces perseverance, character, and hope.
- **2 Corinthians 12:9–10** – God's power is made perfect in weakness.

**Application:** Counselors should help counselees see crisis as a refining fire, drawing them closer to God.

## 6. Case Example: A Family After a Sudden Loss
A family loses their child in a tragic accident. The counselor must:

- Sit with them in silence at first (Job 2:13).
- Remind them of God's nearness (Psalm 34:18).
- Gently direct them to eternal hope in Christ (1 Thessalonians 4:13–14).

- Help them with practical support through the church community.
- Walk with them long-term, not just in the immediate aftermath.

## 7. Christ Our Anchor in Crisis

Jesus Himself endured crises—storms, betrayal, Gethsemane, and the cross. He is the perfect counselor for the suffering.

- **Hebrews 4:15-16** – Christ sympathizes with our weaknesses and invites us to draw near to the throne of grace.
- **John 16:33** – "In the world you will have tribulation; but be of good cheer, I have overcome the world."
- **Hebrews 6:19** – Hope in Christ is an anchor for the soul.

**Application:** Counselors must point counselees to Christ as the unshakable refuge in every storm.

### Conclusion

Crisis shakes foundations, but it also reveals where trust is placed. Biblical counseling in times of crisis is not about clever words but about bringing God's presence, Word, and promises to hurting people.

By showing compassion, grounding counselees in Scripture, meeting practical needs, and pointing them to Christ, the counselor helps turn crisis into a place of spiritual growth and renewed faith.

### Reflection Questions for Chapter 21

1. How do biblical examples like Job, Elijah, and the disciples show different responses to crisis?
2. What promises of God bring comfort in times of trouble (Isaiah 41:10; Psalm 34:17-19)?
3. Why is presence and compassion often more powerful than many words in a crisis (Job 2:13)?
4. How can crisis become an opportunity for spiritual growth

# THE PRINCIPLES OF NOUTHETIC COUNSELING

(Romans 5:3–5; 2 Corinthians 12:9–10)?
5. How does Christ serve as the believer's anchor in crisis (John 16:33; Hebrews 6:19)?

# Chapter 22: Counseling and Spiritual Warfare

**Introduction**

Every counseling situation takes place in the context of a larger battle: the **spiritual warfare** between God's kingdom and the powers of darkness. Many counselees struggle not only with fleshly desires but also with spiritual attacks, temptations, and demonic lies.

Nouthetic counseling equips believers to stand firm in Christ's victory, resist the devil, and live in freedom.

"For we do not wrestle against flesh and blood, but against principalities, against powers, against the rulers of the darkness of this age, against spiritual hosts of wickedness in the heavenly places."
—Ephesians 6:12

**1. The Reality of Spiritual Warfare**

The Bible makes clear that believers face an active enemy.

- **1 Peter 5:8** – The devil prowls around like a roaring lion, seeking whom he may devour.
- **John 10:10** – Satan comes to steal, kill, and destroy.
- **2 Corinthians 11:3** – Satan deceived Eve by cunning, and seeks to corrupt minds.

**Application:** Counselors must help counselees understand that struggles are not merely psychological or circumstantial but often part of a spiritual battle.

**2. The Enemy's Tactics**

Satan's weapons include:

- **Deception** – Twisting God's truth (Genesis 3:1–5; John 8:44).

- **Accusation** – Condemning believers (Revelation 12:10).
- **Temptation** – Enticing to sin (James 1:14–15; Matthew 4:1–11).
- **Fear and intimidation** – Attempting to paralyze faith (2 Timothy 1:7).

**Application:** Counselors must expose the lies counselees believe and replace them with God's truth.

### 3. The Believer's Position in Christ
Victory in spiritual warfare flows from the believer's union with Christ.

- **Colossians 2:13–15** – Christ disarmed principalities and powers at the cross.
- **1 John 4:4** – Greater is He who is in you than he who is in the world.
- **Romans 8:37** – We are more than conquerors through Him who loved us.

**Application:** Counselees must be reminded that they fight not for victory but **from victory** in Christ.

### 4. The Armor of God
Ephesians 6:13–18 provides the believer's defense:

- **Belt of Truth** – Knowing and applying God's Word.
- **Breastplate of Righteousness** – Living in holiness and guarding against guilt.
- **Shoes of the Gospel of Peace** – Standing firm in reconciliation with God.
- **Shield of Faith** – Trusting God to extinguish Satan's fiery darts.
- **Helmet of Salvation** – Assurance of eternal security in

# THE PRINCIPLES OF NOUTHETIC COUNSELING

Christ.
- **Sword of the Spirit** – Using Scripture against lies and temptations.
- **Prayer** – Continual dependence on God in battle.

**Application:** Counselors should help counselees identify which piece of armor they are neglecting and teach them to put it on daily.

## 5. Resisting the Devil

Scripture gives practical commands for resisting Satan's attacks.

- **James 4:7** – Submit to God, resist the devil, and he will flee.
- **1 Peter 5:9** – Resist him, steadfast in the faith.
- **Matthew 4:1-11** – Jesus resisted temptation by quoting Scripture.

**Application:** Counselees must actively resist, not passively give in, standing firm on God's promises.

## 6. The Power of Prayer and Fasting

Prayer is essential in spiritual battle.

- **Matthew 6:13** – Pray for deliverance from the evil one.
- **Ephesians 6:18** – Pray always with all perseverance.
- **Mark 9:29** – Some demonic strongholds are broken only through prayer and fasting.

**Application:** Counselors should teach counselees to cultivate disciplined prayer lives, calling on God's power.

## 7. Case Example: Overcoming Fear of Demonic Attack

A believer fears demonic oppression. The counselor must:

- Teach assurance of Christ's victory (Colossians 2:15).
- Encourage resistance through truth and prayer (James 4:7).
- Help renew the mind with Scriptures on God's protection

(Psalm 91).
- Remind them that Satan's power is limited and defeated.

## 8. The Balance in Spiritual Warfare

While we must not ignore Satan's schemes, we must also avoid exaggerating them.

- **2 Corinthians 2:11** – We are not ignorant of his devices.
- **Colossians 3:2** – Focus on things above, not overly fixated on demonic activity.
- **Hebrews 12:2** – Keep eyes fixed on Jesus, not the devil.

**Application:** Counselors must guide counselees to take Satan seriously but not fearfully—our focus is on Christ's supremacy.

## 9. Christ the Victor

The foundation of all victory is Christ's triumph.

- **Hebrews 2:14–15** – Through death, Jesus destroyed the one who had the power of death.
- **Revelation 12:11** – Believers overcome by the blood of the Lamb and the word of their testimony.
- **Philippians 2:10–11** – Every knee will bow before Christ.

**Application:** Counselors must consistently point counselees back to the finished work of Christ as the source of their strength.

### Conclusion

Spiritual warfare is real, but the believer is not defenseless. God has provided His Word, His Spirit, His armor, and His promises. The counselor's role is to help counselees recognize Satan's schemes, resist with truth, and walk in the victory Christ already secured at the cross.

"Yet in all these things we are more than conquerors through Him who loved us."
—Romans 8:37

## Reflection Questions for Chapter 22

1. What are Satan's primary tactics against believers (Genesis 3:1–5; Revelation 12:10)?
2. How does the believer's union with Christ guarantee victory (Colossians 2:15; 1 John 4:4)?
3. What role does the armor of God play in resisting the enemy (Ephesians 6:13–18)?
4. How can prayer and fasting strengthen believers in spiritual battle (Mark 9:29; Ephesians 6:18)?
5. How does Revelation 12:11 summarize the believer's triumph over Satan?

# Chapter 23: The Goal of Nouthetic Counseling: Christlikeness

**Introduction**

Nouthetic counseling is not simply about solving problems, easing pain, or managing behavior. Its ultimate goal is far higher: **to see believers conformed to the image of Christ.** Every counseling session, every admonition, and every application of Scripture must move the counselee toward greater **holiness, maturity, and Christlikeness.**

"For whom He foreknew, He also predestined to be conformed to the image of His Son."
—Romans 8:29

**1. Christlikeness as God's Eternal Purpose**

God's purpose for every believer is transformation into Christ's image.

- **2 Corinthians 3:18** – We are being transformed into His image from glory to glory by the Spirit.
- **Ephesians 4:13** – The goal of ministry is that we all attain to the fullness of Christ.
- **Colossians 1:28** – Paul counseled and taught every man to present them perfect in Christ Jesus.

**Application:** Counselors must never lose sight that Christlikeness—not comfort—is the end goal of counseling.

**2. Christ as the Model**

Christ is the pattern for life and godliness.

- **Philippians 2:5-8** – Have the same mind of humility as Christ.

- **1 Peter 2:21** – Christ left us an example, that we should follow in His steps.
- **John 13:14–15** – Jesus washed His disciples' feet as an example of service.

**Application:** Counselors should constantly point counselees to Christ's example in humility, obedience, and love.

### 3. The Role of Sanctification

Sanctification is the process by which believers grow in holiness and become more like Christ.

- **1 Thessalonians 4:3** – "This is the will of God, your sanctification."
- **John 17:17** – "Sanctify them by Your truth; Your word is truth."
- **Hebrews 12:10** – God disciplines us so we may share in His holiness.

**Application:** Counseling must emphasize the role of God's Word, Spirit, and discipline in sanctification.

### 4. The Word of God as the Instrument of Change

Christlikeness comes as the Word renews the mind.

- **Romans 12:2** – Be transformed by the renewing of your mind.
- **Psalm 19:7–8** – God's Word revives the soul and makes wise the simple.
- **2 Timothy 3:16–17** – All Scripture equips the man of God for every good work.

**Application:** Counselors must equip counselees with Scripture as the primary tool of transformation.

# THE PRINCIPLES OF NOUTHETIC COUNSELING 137

**5. The Spirit's Power in Transformation**
The Holy Spirit is the agent of change.

- **Galatians 5:22–23** – The fruit of the Spirit reflects Christ's character.
- **Romans 8:13–14** – By the Spirit we put to death the deeds of the body.
- **Philippians 2:13** – God works in us both to will and to do for His good pleasure.

**Application:** Counseling must lead the counselee to dependence on the Spirit, not self-effort.

**6. Growth in Love**
The greatest mark of Christlikeness is love.

- **John 13:34–35** – Love one another as Christ loved you.
- **1 Corinthians 13:4–7** – Love is patient, kind, not self-seeking.
- **1 John 4:16–17** – As Christ is, so are we in this world, perfected in love.

**Application:** The counselor must urge the counselee to measure growth not by knowledge alone but by increasing love for God and others.

**7. Perseverance in Trials**
Christlikeness is forged in the furnace of trials.

- **James 1:2–4** – Trials produce endurance, leading to maturity.
- **Romans 5:3–5** – Tribulation produces perseverance, character, and hope.
- **Hebrews 5:8** – Jesus learned obedience through suffering.

**Application:** Counselors should help counselees embrace trials as God's tools for shaping Christlike character.

### 8. Case Example: From Selfishness to Christlike Love

A counselee struggles with anger and selfishness in marriage. The counselor must:

- Point him to Christ's sacrificial love (Ephesians 5:25).
- Teach him to put off selfish desires and put on service (Philippians 2:3–4).
- Encourage him to walk by the Spirit to bear the fruit of patience and kindness (Galatians 5:22).

Result: Growth in Christlikeness that blesses both his marriage and his witness.

### 9. The Ultimate Hope of Christlikeness

Our transformation will one day be complete.

- **1 John 3:2** – When He appears, we shall be like Him.
- **Philippians 3:20–21** – Christ will transform our lowly body to be like His glorious body.
- **Romans 8:30** – Those whom God justified, He also glorified.

**Application:** Counselors should give hope that present growth leads to the ultimate reality of glorification.

### Conclusion

The ultimate goal of nouthetic counseling is not temporary relief or problem-solving but lasting transformation into the likeness of Christ. Through the Word of God, the work of the Spirit, and the trials of life, believers are being shaped into His image until the day they see Him face to face.

"My little children, for whom I labor in birth again until Christ is formed in you."
—Galatians 4:19

## Reflection Questions for Chapter 23

1. How does Romans 8:29 define God's purpose for believers?
2. In what ways does Christ serve as the model for sanctification (Philippians 2:5-8; 1 Peter 2:21)?
3. How does the Word of God renew the mind and transform lives (Romans 12:2; 2 Timothy 3:16-17)?
4. Why is dependence on the Holy Spirit essential for Christlikeness (Galatians 5:22-23; Philippians 2:13)?
5. How does the hope of future glorification (1 John 3:2) motivate present growth?

# Chapter 24: The Eternal Perspective in Counseling

**Introduction**

Counseling often deals with present struggles—anger, fear, grief, addiction—but Scripture continually points us to something greater: the **eternal perspective**. Without this heavenly vision, believers may lose hope, grow weary, or become consumed with temporary problems.

The eternal perspective reminds us that this world is not our home. Our present sufferings are real, but they are light and momentary compared to the eternal weight of glory that awaits us.

"For our light affliction, which is but for a moment, is working for us a far more exceeding and eternal weight of glory."
—2 Corinthians 4:17

**1. The Temporary Nature of Earthly Trials**

All suffering, no matter how severe, is temporary compared to eternity.

- **Romans 8:18** – "The sufferings of this present time are not worthy to be compared with the glory which shall be revealed in us."
- **1 Peter 1:6** – We are grieved by trials "for a little while."
- **James 4:14** – Life is a vapor that appears for a little time and then vanishes.

**Application:** Counselors must help counselees see beyond the immediacy of pain to the brevity of life.

**2. The Hope of Heaven**

Heaven is the believer's ultimate hope.

- **John 14:1–3** – Jesus prepares a place for us in His Father's

house.
- **Philippians 3:20** – Our citizenship is in heaven.
- **Revelation 21:4** – God will wipe away every tear; no more death, sorrow, crying, or pain.

**Application:** Counselors should encourage counselees to live with eternity in view, longing for the presence of Christ.

**3. Eternal Rewards**
God promises rewards for faithfulness in this life.

- **2 Timothy 4:8** – A crown of righteousness awaits those who love His appearing.
- **1 Corinthians 3:12–15** – Our works will be tested by fire, and faithful service will be rewarded.
- **Matthew 25:21** – "Well done, good and faithful servant."

**Application:** Counselors can motivate counselees by showing that obedience in trials brings eternal reward.

**4. The Resurrection Hope**
The resurrection assures us of victory over death.

- **1 Thessalonians 4:13–18** – Believers will rise to meet the Lord, and we will always be with Him.
- **1 Corinthians 15:52–57** – Death is swallowed up in victory through Christ.
- **John 11:25–26** – Jesus said, "I am the resurrection and the life."

**Application:** The resurrection provides solid hope for counselees facing loss, sickness, or fear of death.

# THE PRINCIPLES OF NOUTHETIC COUNSELING 143

**5. Living with an Eternal Mindset**
Eternal hope transforms daily living.

- **Colossians 3:1-2** – Set your mind on things above, not on things on the earth.
- **Hebrews 12:1-2** – Run with endurance, fixing eyes on Jesus.
- **Matthew 6:19-20** – Store up treasures in heaven, not on earth.

**Application:** Counselors should help believers prioritize eternal values over temporal comfort.

**6. Case Example: Encouraging the Suffering Believer**
A counselee battling cancer fears death. The counselor must:

- Remind them of the temporary nature of suffering (2 Corinthians 4:17).
- Point them to the promise of heaven (Revelation 21:4).
- Assure them of resurrection hope (1 Thessalonians 4:16).
- Encourage them to live faithfully until the end, knowing eternal reward awaits (2 Timothy 4:8).

**7. Christ Our Eternal Hope**
The ultimate focus of eternity is not a place, but a Person—Christ Himself.

- **John 17:24** – Jesus desires that we be with Him and behold His glory.
- **Philippians 1:21-23** – "For to me, to live is Christ, and to die is gain."
- **Revelation 22:3-4** – In eternity, we will see His face and serve Him forever.

**Application:** Counselors must remind counselees that heaven is glorious because Christ is there.

**Conclusion**

The eternal perspective transforms how we face trials, grief, and struggles in this life. It anchors us in hope, sustains us in suffering, and motivates us to live for Christ.

The counselor's task is not merely to relieve present pain but to lift the counselee's eyes to eternity, where every tear will be wiped away, every wound will be healed, and every believer will be conformed perfectly to Christ.

"Looking for the blessed hope and glorious appearing of our great God and Savior Jesus Christ."

—Titus 2:13

**Reflection Questions for Chapter 24**

1. How does 2 Corinthians 4:17–18 reshape the way believers see trials?
2. What promises of heaven bring comfort to the suffering (John 14:1–3; Revelation 21:4)?
3. How do eternal rewards encourage perseverance (1 Corinthians 3:12–15; Matthew 25:21)?
4. Why is the resurrection essential for Christian hope (1 Corinthians 15:52–57)?
5. How can fixing our eyes on Christ (Hebrews 12:2) sustain us in daily struggles?

# Conclusion: The Sufficiency of Christ and His Word

**The Journey of Nouthetic Counseling**

Throughout this book, we have walked through the principles and practices of **Nouthetic Counseling**—biblical confrontation, encouragement, and teaching with the goal of producing lasting change in the lives of God's people.

We have seen how God's Word speaks to every area of life: anger, fear, anxiety, addictions, marriage, grief, depression, forgiveness, and even spiritual warfare. Each chapter has reminded us that the goal of counseling is not mere problem-solving but **conformity to Christ.**

**The Foundation: God's Word**

The bedrock of biblical counseling is the **sufficiency of Scripture.**

- **2 Timothy 3:16–17** – All Scripture is inspired and profitable, equipping us for every good work.
- **Psalm 19:7–8** – God's Word revives the soul, makes wise the simple, and rejoices the heart.

Nouthetic counseling does not rely on human wisdom, psychology, or temporary solutions. It rests entirely on the living, active Word of God (Hebrews 4:12).

**The Power: The Holy Spirit**

True change is impossible without the Spirit's power.

- **Galatians 5:16** – Walk in the Spirit, and you will not fulfill the lust of the flesh.
- **Romans 8:13–14** – By the Spirit we put to death the deeds of the body.

The Spirit applies God's Word, convicts of sin, empowers obedience, and produces Christlike fruit.

### The Process: Sanctification

The biblical process of change follows the pattern of **put off, renew, put on.**

- **Ephesians 4:22–24** – Put off the old man, be renewed in the spirit of your mind, and put on the new man.
- **Colossians 3:8–14** – Put off anger, wrath, malice, and put on compassion, kindness, humility, and love.

Counseling helps counselees recognize sin, replace lies with truth, and cultivate habits of righteousness.

### The Goal: Christlikeness

Every chapter has pointed toward the same ultimate goal—**to see believers conformed to the image of Christ.**

- **Romans 8:29** – Predestined to be conformed to the image of His Son.
- **Colossians 1:28** – Present every person mature in Christ.
- **2 Corinthians 3:18** – Transformed into His image from glory to glory.

The counselor's task is to faithfully guide counselees toward maturity in Christ, not mere outward improvement.

### The Hope: Eternity

Finally, the eternal perspective sustains believers in every struggle.

- **2 Corinthians 4:17** – Present afflictions are light compared to eternal glory.
- **Philippians 3:20** – Our citizenship is in heaven.
- **Revelation 21:4** – God will wipe away every tear.

# THE PRINCIPLES OF NOUTHETIC COUNSELING 147

Counseling must lift the eyes of the hurting beyond the temporary to the eternal, anchoring them in the blessed hope of Christ's return.

**A Word to Counselors**

Dear counselor, your calling is sacred. You are an instrument of God's grace, entrusted with His Word to bring admonition, encouragement, and hope. Counseling is not about your wisdom or strength but about faithfully applying Scripture, prayerfully depending on the Spirit, and lovingly walking with others toward Christlikeness.

Remember:

- Speak truth in love (Ephesians 4:15).
- Be patient with the weak (1 Thessalonians 5:14).
- Restore the fallen with gentleness (Galatians 6:1).
- Always point to Christ, the Wonderful Counselor (Isaiah 9:6).

**Final Exhortation**

The principles of Nouthetic Counseling are not merely techniques but an outworking of the gospel. Christ is the Counselor, His Word is the guide, His Spirit is the power, and His glory is the goal.

May every counselor and counselee find their hope, strength, and transformation in Him alone.

"Now may the God of peace Himself sanctify you completely; and may your whole spirit, soul, and body be preserved blameless at the coming of our Lord Jesus Christ. He who calls you is faithful, who also will do it."

—1 Thessalonians 5:23-24

**About the Author**

**Dr. Greg Wood** is a pastor, teacher, and biblical counselor with a passion for applying God's Word to the needs of His people. With years of ministry experience in preaching, teaching, and counseling,

Dr. Wood has dedicated his life to equipping believers to live in the power of God's truth.

He writes and teaches with the conviction that the Bible is fully sufficient for all matters of life and godliness (2 Peter 1:3), and that true transformation comes through the Spirit of God working with the Word of God in the people of God.

**Final Exhortation to Readers**

Dear reader, may this book not simply inform your mind, but transform your ministry and life. Remember that true counseling is not about human wisdom but about faithfully pointing others to Christ, who is the Wonderful Counselor (Isaiah 9:6).

Walk humbly, counsel biblically, and trust that God's Word is powerful enough to bring change.

# Don't miss out!

Visit the website below and you can sign up to receive emails whenever Dr. Greg Wood publishes a new book. There's no charge and no obligation.

https://books2read.com/r/B-A-GGWME-KLGXG

BOOKS 2 READ

Connecting independent readers to independent writers.

www.ingramcontent.com/pod-product-compliance
Lightning Source LLC
Chambersburg PA
CBHW022105160426
43198CB00008B/357